D0030232

On Becoming
Pottywise
for Toddlers

Books in this Series

On Becoming Birthwise
On Becoming Babywise
On Becoming Babywise II
On Becoming Toddlerwise
On Becoming Preschoolwise
On Becoming Childwise
On Becoming Preteenwise
On Becoming Teenwise

ON BECOMING

POTTYWISE
FOR TODDLERS

---

*A developmental
readiness approach to
potty training*

GARY EZZO, M.A. AND
ROBERT BUCKNAM, M.D.

ON BECOMING POTTYWISE FOR TODDLERS

® *"ON BECOMING" is a registered Trademark*

Published by Parent-Wise Solutions, Inc.
(A division of the Charleston Publishing Group, Inc.)

© 2005 by Gary Ezzo and Robert Bucknam, M.D.
Illustrations by Cynthia Gardner
pixelworksstudio.net

International Standard Book Number: 1-932740-14-7

Printed in the United States of America

ALL RIGHTS RESERVED
No part of this publication may be reproduced, stored in a retrieval
system, or transmitted in any form or by any means—electronic,
mechanical, photocopying, recording, or otherwise—without prior
written permission.

For information:
Parent-Wise Solutions, Inc.
2130 Cheswick Lane, Mt. Pleasant, SC 29466

PRINT
05 07 09 10 11
- - - - -
1   2   3   4   5

Dedicated to:

Tom and Dawn Randall
True Friends and
faithful warriors

ACKNOWLEDGMENTS

Books are often a collaborative effort of many individuals whose gifts and talents help move a manuscript from scribbles to completion. This little book on a big topic is no exception. In general, we wish to thank our educational consultants and pediatric advisors for their insights and assistance in putting this helpful tool in the hands of so many parents. This includes Dr. Jim Pearson and Dr. Rusty Terner. We also wish to thank Stacy Miller and Stephanie Taylor for the wonderful contributions to this book. Their work was supplemented by those of Deirdre Salmon, Jenice Hoffman, and Carla Link. Other contributors include Susan St. Clair, Pam Standly, Luona Nightingale, Shannon Herring, Julie Young, Dana Ott, Carol Mohr, Pamela S. Ramont, Cyndi Birds, Tracy Burner, Roni Hathaway, Anne Ratliff, Jocelyn Schumacher, Jeana Owens, Karen Kurtz, and Karen Forden. Finally, many thanks to Judith St. Pierre, PhD, for her marvelous handling of the text.

CONTENTS

PREFACE

Do the math: If a mother averages six diaper changes a day, she'll change approximately 2,190 diapers during her baby's first year. Things improve slightly over the next twelve months. Based on five changes a day, she'll add another 1,825 diaper changes to her score. By the time her child is half-way to her third birthday, Mom will pass the 5,000 mark. That's a lot of dirty diapers! If this mom is you, it's no wonder you're thinking seriously about potty training.

Back in the 1960s, the prevalent use of cloth diapers made the decision to potty train easy. Days of washing and bleaching and hanging out the laundry was a strong incentive to train early. Mom had better things to do, and usually by age two, the diaper gig was up. Today, with disposable diapers potty training is more relaxed and that is better for the child. Still, if you're holding this book in your hand, you're probably ready to get started.

While successful potty training in itself is not considered a developmental milestone in a child's life, it is nonetheless an important transition for both you and your child. This book is based on the simple fact that toilet training is a skill that children must learn early in life. All parents know this. It's a journey children must take with mom and dad navigating the way. But where do you begin? Is your child old enough to interpret and properly respond to the new sensations associated with elimination? What signs do you look for? What equipment do you need? How do you keep your little person focused? How do you motivate her to use the potty instead of her diaper and, once she achieves success, keep her going on her own? The answers to these questions and many more are only a few pages away.

The good news is that potty training doesn't have to be complicated—and neither does a book that explains it. Busy moms need a resource that gives them comprehensive information without a lot of unnecessary details and presents them with options instead of a one-size-fits-all program. *On Becoming Pottywise for Toddlers* provides all of that and more.

In addition and acting on the advice of our counseling moms, we adapted a chapter from our book *On Becoming Toddlerwise* and incorporated it as an Appendix entitled: "Structuring Your Toddler's Day." Like so many other aspects of training and educating children, structure and routine are native allies to learning and healthy growth. A routine enhances good organization, time management and provides order. It helps you to achieve your personal goals for your child, while meeting all of his or her needs. Without a doubt structure and routine is a friend to any mom preparing to potty train her toddler. We know this addition will be a great parenting resource for many months to come.

Finally, *On Becoming Pottywise for Toddlers* replicates the early work done by Gary and Anne Marie Ezzo in their book *Potty Training 1-2-3*. It was the author's and publisher's desire to reintroduce these training precepts in this second book to reach the needs of a wider audience more familiar with the *On Becoming* series of books.

With all that said, it is time to get started. Happy training.

Gary Ezzo, M.A.
Robert Bucknam, M.D.

Chapter One

Understanding Readiness

Kimber placed her black saddle purse on the table and took a seat. Parents, mostly moms, were sitting at tables around the room chatting while they waited for the class to begin. April, Mary, and Alicia were already seated at table two. Each possessed a warm Southern smile and attentive eyes that greeted Kimber like an old friend.

"Hey, Kimber," Mary said, "How did things go with Jaclyn Lee?"

Kimber smiled and momentarily pondered the question, reflecting on the day she had first considered the possibility. *"Could it really be this easy? If I could get it done in one day…"* Her eyes searched out her inquirer.

"Jaclyn was potty trained in less than five hours. She picked out her favorite doll, I put her in pants and walked her through the process a couple of times, and by noon the mission was accomplished. It worked just as they said it would—one, two, three."

Alicia eyed her skeptically. "No way, Kimber," she said, her tone more hopeful than incredulous. "Was it really that easy?"

Her words trailed off as the attention of the room shifted toward the movement at the door. "Hey, Allyson," someone called out, "How did it go with Jackson?" Allyson held up the index finger of her right hand.

"One week?" Alicia asked, her eyes now fixed on Allyson.

"No," Allyson said. "One day. Jackson was potty trained by four o'clock last Friday afternoon."

April, Mary, and Alicia looked at each other. "I don't know about you," Mary said, "but I'm starting tomorrow!" Encouraged and resolute, April and Alicia nodded.

Kimber's and Allyson's success can be your success or at least something close to it. While we can not make any promises, we can tell you that many of the moms we work with achieve the potty training success they hope for in a day or two. Others accomplish their goals in three to seven days. What made *On Becoming Pottywise for Toddlers* principals work for these moms? It was the combination of right timing, right method, and right motivation.

1. **Timing:** They learn to recognize the optimal time for training their toddlers.

2. **Education:** They learn the most effective ways to teach the potty training process.

3. **Motivation:** They learn how to sustain their toddlers' excitement about using the potty.

What Are You Waiting For?

Are you waiting for advice from experts to get started? As long as there are toddlers, potty training advice will abound. A Yahoo search of those two words on the Internet turned up 446,000 links. Not surprisingly, a review of the first 20 links showed that there's a wide variety of opinions on the subject. What was once considered just a common transition of childhood early training has now become the cornerstone of some interesting but equally doubtful psychological theories.

Dr. Sigmund Freud, the "Father of Psychoanalysis," assumed that any conflict involving potty training would damage a child's developing psyche and carry over into adulthood. We're not sure what that theory looks like in practice since there are very few examples among the worlds adult population of abnormal bathroom usage. It is difficult for researchers to confirm this theory. Others, who piggybacked their own theories on Freud's assumptions, have added to a growing paranoia about potty training—one which, in our opinion, has more to do with the parent's psyche than the child's. How helpful is the advice based on such theories?

Referring to Freud, Dr. Burton L. White says that "such theoretical analysis has never been supported by evidence." He goes on to explain: "Given what we know today, no justification exists for elaborate treaties of dire concern about toilet training. It is simply one of a large number of necessary chores that are required of all parents."[1] Even though Dr. White made these comments some

---

[1] Burton L. White, MD, *The New First Three Years of Life* (New York: Simon & Schuster, 1985), 325–6.

18 years ago, his views continue to reflect those of mainstream pediatricians.

Although many different people, all wonderfully qualified to be experts, helped shape the concepts in this book, we have drawn heavily upon mothers whose success in potty training qualifies them to speak on this subject with as much authority as any theorist of the past or present. In the political world of toddlers, these moms would be considered *centrist*. All shared a common goal of moving their toddlers from diapers to daytime and nighttime dryness. And while their methods varied from family to family, they shared a common starting point—their child's *developmental readiness*. In life there is a time and a place for everything. The time for potty training is set by the child's developmental clock; that is what you're waiting for—*the readiness factor*. The place is set by Mom.

Developmental Readiness

Picture two-year-old Katie in her fuzzy pink sweater and matching mittens as she approaches the ice for her first skating lesson. With the family video running, the blue-eyed cutie is all giggles and gaiety—until she takes that first slippery step on the ice and promptly falls on her bottom. Cut the camera. Along with her parents' dream of Olympic gold, Katy has come undone, and nothing can get her back on the ice. Planet Earth to Kate's folks: Save the big bucks for later. The child is simply not ready for ice-skating.

It's the same with potty training. Of the many universal laws of child development, one in particular has specific application for the sport of potty training. It's called the *structure-function principle*, and it states that a child cannot perform certain functions (activities), until specific developmental structures are in place and sufficiently mature. This is a fancy way of saying don't start training your child until she has both the capacity to learn and the ability to achieve.

Does this sound a bit confusing? It's not. We'll take this readiness thing step by step, and in a couple of pages you'll be thoroughly familiar with all the processes involved. Why do you need to know these things? Because understanding how all the pieces fit together will help you find the training strategy that is right for you and your child. Keep in mind that not all of the developmental components necessary for successful potty training must be matured before you begin (including neurological, muscular, hormonal, emotional, and volitional components of growth), but they will all have reached maturity by the time your child is fully trained.

Finally, please govern your training by this single principal: *Every child is different.* Just because little Sarah Lynn next door potty trained at 24 months doesn't mean that your Shelley Lou will be ready then as well. Nor does it guarantee that Sarah Lynn's little brother will be able to repeat his sister's success. All children reach the point of developmental readiness for potty training, but they do not all arrive at the same time.

Understanding *Dry* and *Clean*

For any parent deeply involved in the potty project, dry and clean means one thing: freedom. No more carting off a messy munchkin to a private location to wipe and powder and lift and fit. Dry and clean are beautiful ideas to behold, and "Mommy, I have to go potty" is music to the ear.

For the child, however, dry and clean represents a different kind of triumph. In the broadest sense, it means that her brain and body have mastered the ability to control the bladder and bowel producing the wonderful results of dry and clean. *Dry* refers to bladder training mastery, while *clean* refers to bowel training mastery. When both are achieved, the child is "toilet trained."

Many parents assume that dry and clean are part of the same physical process. That is not true. Bladder and bowel training are connected only in that they are part of the overall elimination process and that potty training in general speaks to both activities. The connection between the two stop there because they involve different sensations and different muscles. They are two distinct arenas of training.

Bladder control is more complex because many more neurological and physiological components must mature before true potty training is achieved. In contrast, the only specific readiness cue for bowel training is the child's ability to sit up-right in a chair (which she can do before her first birthday), and her mother's desire to start training. For this reason, we'll focus first on bladder readiness, starting with an explanation of its function.

Bladder Readiness

The bladder is amazing. Consider for a moment how this muscle works. During the digestive process, foods and liquids are separated from bulk waste. The liquids are directed to the kidneys for filtering, and the bulk continues through the colon for discharge. In adults, the kidneys filter approximately 200 quarts of fluid each day. Of that, 198 quarts are returned to the bloodstream, while 2 quarts of filtered waste are sent to the bladder.

Minute by minute, much like a slow I.V. drip, urine from the kidneys passes through the ureters to the bladder. Most of this takes place without our being aware of it since we have no sensation of the bladder filling, at least not until its walls begin to stretch. When that happens, "stretch-receptor" nerves begin to send faint signals to the brain to let us know that we need to urinate. As that signal grows stronger, we become conscious of the need. Through training and conditioning, we have learned how to control our bladder muscles until we find a socially acceptable place to go. At the appropriate time and place that we are free to relieve ourselves, we authorize the brain to send a message to contract the bladder wall and relax the sphincter muscle. We then release our urine.

The process works differently during infancy. Early in a baby's life, a neurological autopilot in the brain handles the "full bladder" message. When the bladder fills to a certain level, your baby's bladder muscles automatically contract, releasing the urine through the sphincter muscle. This is a reflex emptying, not a cognitive experience, and it continues to control the elimination of urine for the first year and-a-half of life.

Researchers have not yet determined the exact moment when the neurological autopilot switches off and the bladder message system switches on. Theoretical evidence (and just about every grandmother), suggests that the change takes place sometime between 18 and 22 months of age. Once the neurological switch is turned on, training opportunities are on the horizon. This does not mean your child is ready for training however. More time is needed for the nerves that signal the bladder sensation and enable a child to manage her bladder and sphincter muscles to mature before she can voluntarily control elimination. This means that true bladder mastery may still be months away.

Three phases of bladder readiness

For all toddlers, the sequence of bladder development for all toddlers starts with the *awakening* phase, then advances to the *mediating* phase, and concludes with the *educational* phase. Every child passes through this sequence, although the speed at which their minds and bodies navigate the process differs from child to child, and even between girls and boys. Some children move through the three phases by 24 months of age, while others arrive at full readiness at 36 months or later. Remember our first principal, every child is different!

The awakening phase usually begins between 18 and 24 months. At some point, your child awakens to a new sensation—*bladder pressure*. She recognizes the pressure but is not fully aware of what it means or what to do with it. The second phase (mediating), comes into play between 22 to 32 months. This is when your child becomes aware that she can control the release of her urine. She now associates a cause and effect, mainly the pressure, then sensation of urinating, followed by the uncomfortable feeling of a wet diaper. As a result, the mediating phase produces very definite signs of readiness. Your daughter stops an activity, does her business, tugs on her diaper, and wants you to change her right away.

The educational phase of training involves learning what to do with her sensation other than releasing her urine in her diaper. This includes learning how to check herself for dryness, how to pull her pants down and sit, release her urine in the potty and eventually learn how to clean-up after herself. She will not naturally know these things; you must teach her what is expected.

Daytime vs. nighttime bladder readiness

Daytime bladder readiness is one thing; nighttime readiness is another. Nighttime dryness usually requires more time to develop. Normally, when a child acquires the ability to interpret the bladder message (the mediating phase), her bladder can hold urine for two to four hours. This is one reason she doesn't stay dry through the night. Her bladder must continue growing to the point to store concentrated urine for eight to ten hours. In addition, the brain-to-bladder wake reflex must have time to mature, allowing her to wake out of a sound sleep when her bladder is full.

Finally, there's the release of the *antidiuretic hormone* (ADH) that helps slow the production of urine. The body normally produces more ADH at night in order to reduce the need to urinate. If the body doesn't produce enough of it, the bladder can fill and bedwetting may occur.

With all these variables, no wonder it's so difficult to predict exactly when a child will achieve nighttime bladder mastery. We only know that statistically it occurs sometime between 24 and

42 months and certain developmental factors influencing the outcome lay outside of mom and dad's and the child's control.

When does it all come together? We use an 8/18 formula. Sometime between 24 and 32 months (an 8-month period), most children achieve daytime bladder readiness. Sometime between 24 and 42 months (an 18-month period), most children reach nighttime bladder readiness.

These statistics lead to one obvious conclusion: It's not only possible, but also very likely that your toddler can be day trained at 24 months but not night trained until 36 months or later. It's also possible to have one child who is day and night trained by 26 months, while another doesn't even start day training until 36 months. While you may be hoping for faster and more consistent results, each scenario falls well within the "normal" range of achievement and development.

Signs of Readiness

The wheels are coming off. A few months ago, five-year-old Billy noticed that he was the only kid on the block with three wheels on the back of his bike. Since then he has asked his Dad every day, "Can I do it, Dad? Today, Dad, huh?" Today is the day, and Dad is out on the street hanging on to the seat while the brave young peddler wobbles to and fro.

A child's interest in and anticipation for acquiring any developmental skill signals the mediating phase. This is when your child starts showing signs of developmental readiness and also an interest in staying dry and clean. Recognizing that your child is in this second phase of development is key to successful potty training.

How will you know when your child is ready for training? Here are some of the primary and secondary signs.

Primary signs of readiness emerge when your toddler:

- Stays dry for two or more hours at a time.

- Has regular bowel movements.

- Wakes up from her naps dry.

- Stops an activity while urinating or messing in her diaper.

- Stands a certain way and holds on to her diaper as she eliminates.

- Is interested in "big girl" training pants.

- Wants to imitate parents or older siblings using the toilet.

- Is able to understand and follow simple directions.

Secondary signs of readiness emerge when your toddler:

- Can sit and play quietly for about five minutes.

- Can put toys and other possessions where they belong on her own.

- Can dress and undress herself.

- Has a name for urine and bowel movements.[2]

Do all these signs need to be present before you get under way? No, but most of them should be. The more the better, for they will help you avoid the most common mistake parents make, which is to push the educational phase ahead of the mediating phase. Here, parents walk their child through all the how-to's of potty training before she is fully able to relate to the sensations. We have heard it before, and so have you. A mom starts potty training her 22 month old, and while the child has some success, she also has many accidents. Mom concludes the daughter is not catching on.

She's right. The child is not catching on because she's most likely still in the awakening phase of development. Mom should stop, wait a couple of months, and then begin again. Her daughter needs time to physically catch up to Mom's expectations. Attempting to train a child before she is squarely in the mediating phase will only frustrate the child and delay successful training. It doesn't matter how much you put into her little mind, nothing can happen until her little body is ready. But once her body is ready, the educational process may begin.

---

[2]It's a good idea to use the common words "poop," "pee," or "potty." Don't use overly technical language or descriptions that might offend others or embarrass your child in front of others.

Volitional Readiness

Your child's ability and volitional choice to comply is the wild card variable in training. A perverse will can spoil the process. While your child might be physically capable and smart enough to understand what's expected, she must also be a willing participant in her training. Potty training for bladder control is all about integrating the child's ability to recognize bladder sensations with her will to control those sensations. Once she's able to receive the bladder message and control the appropriate muscles, she must *choose* to exercise her newly acquired skills and elect to go in the potty instead of in her pants.

Think of it this way: A child who refuses to follow instructions for tasks she understands will probably not follow instructions for one she knows nothing about. How would you rate your two year old? Does she accept your guidance during the day? Does she eat what you serve her at mealtime without insisting on a new menu? Will she stay put and play for fifteen minutes at a time? When you say, "Don't touch," does she comply? When you call her, does she respond positively, at least 60 percent of the time, or does she throw a fit?

If you can answer yes to most of these questions, potty training will not only be easier, but you can also accomplish it in a day or so. If you answered most of these questions "no", you can still potty train, but the process will be more difficult and take longer. We conclude this based on a simple, self-evident truth: If you have to fight just to get your child's attention, and then do further battle to keep her focused on a task, potty training will not be easy. The process requires her to have a measure of success with both skills.[3]

Mommy Readiness

Now that you've assessed your child's readiness, take a moment to assess your own. Are *you* ready? Are you resolved to avoid false starts and see the process through to the end? While unplanned circumstances may put a temporary halt to your potty training, such interruptions should be the exception.

A false start happens whenever a parent gears up a child's emotions and expectations, begins the process of training, and then loses steam a few days later. This can happen if you're not really ready to begin. Like so many other challenges in parenting, success depends on perseverance. Children pick up cues from their parents. Your child will sense your resolve, or lack of it, during the process. If she senses that you're not committed to the process, she will respond accordingly. That alone can make a big difference.

You can begin training whenever your child is physically ready (she is able to achieve mastery), volitionally ready (she wants to achieve mastery), and educationally ready (she knows what she needs to know to achieve mastery). However, none of this will matter if you have second thoughts while you're buckling up for the ride. So strap yourself in, remain seated, and keep your arms open for hugs at all times. You'll both need plenty of those.

---

[3]To learn more about the benefits of a general routine and how to establish a basic daytime routine for your toddler, see Gary Ezzo and Robert Bucknam, *On Becoming Toddlerwise* (Louisiana, Mo.: Parent-Wise Solutions, 2003), which has an entire chapter devoted to helping parents establish structure and routine for toddlers.

Chapter Two

Starter Basics

*N*ow that you're both ready for the ride, it's time to start your engines. While potty *readiness* begins with the child, potty *training* starts with the parents. You know by the signals she's sending that your child is physically ready and well into the mediating phase, but now it's up to you to decide when to begin, to purchase the equipment you need, and to do a few pretraining warm-up exercises.

The Importance of Timing

The most important thing to keep in mind when starting potty training is to avoid false starts. Although no parent plans to have their potty training efforts thwarted by daily disruptions, they are inevitable if you start your training under any of these conditions:

- You or your child is sick or recovering from an illness.

- You are about to move or have just completed a major move.

- You are in any relational transition, such as the death of a loved one.

- You are in the midst of an unresolved family crisis.

- You are having houseguests for an extended period.

- Mom is in the early months of pregnancy.

Another consideration is whether both parents work. Potty training suffers under part-time management and a stop-and-start attitude. Mom or Dad need to be available for as long as it takes to implement the training strategy. With this in mind, plan on starting when:

- You are able to set aside the time needed to make potty training a priority.

- You have the emotional and practical support of your spouse.

- You are not in a major house transition, job transfer, or renovation project.

The Basics

Like a woman spinning wool, potty training can be poetry in motion if you have the right equipment. When you actually count dollar for dollar, potty training is a relatively inexpensive activity compared to laying out money each week for disposable diapers. Let's face it, all too soon you'll need the money you've been spending on diapers for piano lessons, summer camp, and braces. For now, splurge a little on training equipment. Basic preparation requires only a few items, none of which are very expensive.

Potty chair

New or used? That is often the first question asked. When you consider what a potty chair is used for, collecting human waste, you might want to consider how much it's worth in the overall scheme of things. We found that store and Internet prices are comparable when you add in the Internet shipping charges. New chairs start around $10.00 and go up from there depending on how many bells and whistles you desire.

The "you" in the last sentence refers to Mom and Dad because your child really doesn't have a preference at this early age what her potty chair will look like or what fancy sounds it can make. When looking for a potty chair, don't forget to check the neighborhood. Some great bargains are often found at yard sales.

If you have a multi-level home, consider picking up two potty chairs. Two chairs will make your life easier, especially in time of an urgent potty need. Finally, if you're training a son, make sure the seat comes with the removable splashguard. That little piece of plastic will save you frustration and considerable time in cleanup and unwanted spray.

Potty seat

A workable substitute for the potty chair is the potty seat. They also come in a variety of styles and price ranges starting around $7.00. A potty seat is convenient and easy to use because it fits right over the standard toilet seat. Many children train on the seat without ever visiting a potty chair.

Two features to look for in a basic seat is its design that allows for easy storage or travel, and a splashguard for little boys. The one major disadvantage is its limitation. It works only where there is a toilet, whereas a potty chair can be used in any room and with less supervision[4]. Nonetheless, potty seats provide a workable alternative to potty chairs although the chair, in our opinion, is still highly favored.

Training pants

Potty training assumes you are ready to move a child out of diapers and into either cotton or disposable training pants. We favor traditional cotton pants, since they have a sponge like absorbent core. Training pants with vinyl outer linings works well because the child can feel the wetness when she has an accident, but the urine doesn't escape through the pant's lining. Of course, some sensation of wetness is a good thing since it makes the child feel uncomfortable. Once she realizes the cause-and-effect relationship between the elimination of urine and the subsequent discomfort of feeling wet, she will make great strides in controlling the outcome.

You may have heard the debate concerning disposable training pants versus cotton training pants. The major contention here is whether disposable pants provide the familiar feel of diapers and thus, diminishing a child's reliance on using the potty. Moms who use disposable training pants tell us they find no evidence of this. Their children move just as quickly to potty training mastery

---

[4]A good internet resource to visit is <u>pottytrainingsolutions.com</u>. This mother friendly website offers a variety of products and related helps to assist you with the training process.

without experiencing any setbacks. The key in using disposable pants in training is staying alert to the child's needs.

Potty training dolls

A potty training doll helps maximize learning by combining a toddler's developing imagination and play with a real life experience. It provides the child the opportunity to walk through the training process step by step, not as a student, but as the doll's tutor. In the process of teaching her little friend all the steps of potty training, your toddler learns everything she needs to know. There's no question about this training aid. Helping to direct and influence a positive outcome for the doll greatly enhances the child's personal achievement.

We use the word "doll" generically. A teddy bear that can wear size 2T training pants will work just as well—and perhaps even better. We say that for a couple of reasons. First, teddy bears are gender neutral and so attract both boys and girls. Second, Mr. Teddy can wear the same training pants as your toddler. This is something new and exciting for a child and wearing the same pants will help hold her attention and keep her focused. If a teddy bear is not an option, consider a doll from your child's toy box. The point is, almost anything can work because toddlers possess wonderful imaginations.

Do you need a doll that wets? Not really. But if you're inclined to get an anatomically correct, drink-and-wet, gender-sensitive potty training doll, figure on spending between $15 to $40 dollars, or even more. A good substitute is a Raggedy Ann doll ($10 to $12). Being able to remove the doll's pants is a necessary component of the educational process, and Raggedy Ann has removable pants under her dress. Unfortunately, Raggedy Andy's pants don't come off.

Snack rewards

Since potty training is a skill, goal incentives should be used to reinforce positive behavior. Rewards definitely help do this, so have available a plentiful supply of small treats like M&M candies, raisins, apple slices, or whatever is appropriate for your child. We discuss the proper timing and use of snack rewards in chapter four.

Sippy cup

The sippy cup is not for your child's personal use but for the child's play-time with her training doll. It doesn't have to be fancy, just something your child can manage.

Before Training Commences

Let's go through the checklist. Your child is ready, you are ready and you have everything you need. Now consider introducing your training by bringing out the potty chair. Place it in a common area. The idea is to get your child acquainted with its purpose, which includes the experience of sitting on it. You might even have her sit, diaper off, while watching a potty training video. Who knows? This may lead to a wonderful "accident," worthy of immediate praise and reward.

Potty training is one of those skills where the more a child is able to do for herself, the better. With that in mind, it makes sense to teach your child how to dress and undress herself. Most importantly, she needs to know how to pull down and pull up her pants and underpants and clean herself. All of this will come in time with practice and a considerable amount of patience on Mom and Dad's part.

While you're spending time getting ready, make it a point to enlist a few cheerleaders. After two-and-a-half year-old Brandi has pulled in for a pit stop and used the potty to stay dry, she needs to hear the applause of her biggest fans. Contact a few significant friends and relatives. Let them know that your toddler is starting the potty training process and ask them to be on her encouragement team. To hear praise from Mom and Dad is great, and there should be plenty of it, but hearing it from Grandma, or Uncle Bill, or Miss Nancy next door multiplies your child's excitement and sense of accomplishment. It also helps her learn that potty training is important not just to Mom and Dad, but to all the people who love her.

Chapter Three

Where to Begin?

*I*n a moment we'll get down to the nuts and bolts of potty training and the various strategies that can move your child from a daily regimen of wet and dirty diapers to a routine of dry and clean pants. But first, there's one more decision to make. Which do you target first—bowel or bladder training?

By and large, parents have a single goal in potty training: a *dry* and *clean* child. But these are two very different physiological outcomes. Children do not achieve success at both simultaneously or with the same amount of effort because elimination is not a single activity. Instead, it involves the coordinated use of two distinct muscle groups that your toddler cannot see or imagine. In order to know where to begin training, you need to know the physiology involved and what that means for your child.

How the Various Muscles Work

Here are some important physiological facts to understand and consider before you start your training. First, two different muscle groups and two different sequences control bowel and bladder elimination. Like an adult, a child uses a release-then-push sequence for bladder elimination and a push-then-release sequence for bowel elimination.

In the case of the bladder, a full sensation is followed by release of the sphincter muscle. The child just needs to release the muscle and her urine comes out. Only when her bladder is nearly empty does she sense her need to push out those few remaining drops. Her bowel action is just the opposite. In bowel control, pushing comes first, followed by release.[5] Therefore, bladder training and bowel training are different as they relate to a child adjusting to the sensation of release and push.

What Your Child Must Learn

Remember how simple you thought driving a car was before you actually got behind the wheel? Probably as a teenager you saw your mom or dad point the car in a direction, step on the gas, and move forward. They made smooth turns using only the index finger of one hand. And then your big day came. You sat in the driver's seat only to discover that learning to drive wasn't as easy as it looked. It required mental and physical coordination and practice using different muscles. You pushed the gas pedal one moment and pump the brakes the next. You learned to watch for cars turning or pulling alongside of you. It took some time before you mastered driving and only after you were able to coordinate all the skills needed to drive safely.

---

[5]Sometimes, as with diarrhea, release is the only function, but this is not the norm.

Potty training for a child is much like learning to drive is for a teen. It looks easy, but it's not because it involves learning to coordinate a totally new set of skills. Think about what your toddler has to go through. Before she can achieve mastery, she must not only be aware of the need to eliminate, but also have the ability to resist the urge to go just any time or place. She must learn how to release urine and bowel movements into the toilet by using unseen and unfamiliar muscles that either hold back or release a full bladder or bowel. She must also be able to communicate her need to go to the bathroom. Consolidating all of these skills takes time and generous amounts of patience on the part of Mom and Dad. Here are some specific things a child must learn to do.

Adjust to the sensation

Once a child recognizes the bladder message, she must learn what it feels like to release urine some place other than in a diaper. Stephanie Taylor, one of our contributing moms, writes:

> I knew our younger daughter was making the association when she got up out of the bathtub and asked me to put a diaper on her because she had to go "pee pee." She knew what her body needed to do, and she knew where it needed to be done. Our first challenge was helping her transfer the association from the diaper to the potty chair. Once that was accomplished, we had to help her adjust to the change in the sensation. She was use to urinating with the diaper next to her body, and initially she was afraid to release her urine without the presence

35

of a diaper. The sensation was new, different, and unfamiliar, so she didn't like it. But in time, she adjusted, and we made it through the process just fine.

Recognize muscle control

Once your child has adjusted to the sensation, she needs to understand the muscle control involved. A child doesn't instinctively understand that she can control the muscles that hold and release her waste, and it can take some time to learn this. However, after a few successful trips to the potty, all that may be needed to turn on the light bulb in her little head is a simple statement like "Make the pee-pee come out." Once she does, you'll see wonderful results, as well as a big grin on your toddler's face.

The recognition of bowel control comes more easily and naturally because children have to make some effort to push. For most parents, the challenge is getting their child to do that in the potty. Once a child recognizes the urge, has adjusted to the new sensation, and understands that she controls the muscles, it's just a matter of patience on your part and practice on hers. Children need many opportunities to practice using those muscles at the right time and in an appropriate place.

Bowel Training First

By the time most toddlers are 20 months old, bowel elimination is often regular, while bladder function remains irregular. And for most toddlers, bowel movements are considerably less frequent than urination. Also, the bowel signal usually allows a child more time to react than the bladder signal, and it's also easier for her to control a solid mass than a liquid. With a minimal amount of observation, most parents can predict when their toddler will have a bowel movement. And for that reason some parents prefer to start bowel training first, as is the case with our Asian moms. Here, a fresh perspective might be helpful.

For example, consider the concept of buying a bouquet of flowers in Paris only to carry them around upside down! At least to us Americans, the bouquet is upside down. But to Parisians, holding the flowers face-down just makes sense. The water remains in the stem until the blooms can be supplied by a supporting vase. In potty training, such reverse thinking can apply to the Asian preference of bowel training first. To this part of the world's population, it just makes sense.

Many of our Asian associates train their children this way with great success and very little stress because messy habits never have time to get established. In some Asian cultures children are bowel trained as early as 12 months. Bladder training in contrast, follows only when all signs of day readiness are present, usually after 22 months. In actual practice, of course, the child is not so much trained in bowel control as the parents are trained in predicting their child's daily movements. Knowing their child is ready to have a bowel movement, she is placed on the potty. When the child goes, she begins to integrate a cause-and-effect behavior that would not be present if no training were occurring. Still, her success on the potty is due to Mom's planning, not hers.

Since you have chosen to read *On Becoming Pottywise for Toddlers*, we assume that you're working with a toddler instead of an infant.

Even so, you can achieve the same outcome with your child. The same principle that applies to a baby in Beijing will work with a toddler in Tallahassee. At some point between infancy and early toddlerhood, your child will stop having bowel movements at random times, including at night, and transition to having one or two at fairly regular times during the day. Because of this, you'll be able to predict with a great deal of accuracy your child's "normal" time of bowel elimination and keep her clean by putting her on the potty.

Like our Asian mothers, you are mainly getting your child familiar with going in the potty instead of in her diaper. Repetitive in nature, this type of training instills habits that eventually lead to an acquired skill. The idea here is to get your child accustomed to eliminating in the potty and staying clean, so that a messy diaper becomes abnormal and uncomfortable for her.

Advantages of bowel training first

The rewards of this kind of training can be huge for both you and your child. Consider the following advantages.

1. For Mom, bowel training provides a welcome relief from what most consider the worst part of potty training—changing messy diapers or pants. Since toddlers on average usually go just twice a day, you can eliminate half the messes that require cleaning even if you catch only one bowel movement a day.

2. Your child gains a sense of personal accomplishment when she releases her waste into a potty instead of her diaper.

3. It also prepares her to release her urine into the potty. While she's having a bowel movement, she will often also release her bladder, reinforcing the overall habit of using the potty. From there it is a short step to complete bladder and bowel control.

4. Another advantage is that bowel training can take place simultaneously with other activities, such as during story time or at mealtime. Eating is a pleasurable activity that often takes 20 to 30 minutes. Having your child sit on a booster potty chair at that time is an option, although not necessarily the best, as it raises other issues involving siblings, privacy, and discretion. But if this is the time your child's biological clock goes to work, then take advantage of it.

If you find it distasteful to have your child sit on a potty chair at mealtime, make sure she sits immediately after her meal. To do so is to take advantage of the *gastrocolic reflex*—the peristaltic wave in the colon induced by food entering the stomach. Routinely having her sit increases the chance of your child releasing into the potty with some regularity.

Disadvantages of Bowel Training First

The disadvantages to starting with bowel training are few, but noteworthy.

1. Making this approach work demands vigilance and consistency. You cannot train one day and skip the next.

2. Since the times are fairly fixed when a child will have a bowel movement, some moms feel very confined by the process. It does require a morning and noontime ritual, and there is no substitute for this. Someone has to be there to get the child ready, oversee the process, and clean up the mess afterwards.

3. Because so much emphasis is placed on catching the child in the act of going, her actual understanding of voluntary bowel control might be lost or delayed in the process. The fact is, one or two successes at the potty do not guarantee the child has learned to control her bowel muscles. Perhaps she went this morning because she happened to be sitting on the potty and you caught her at the right time. It might take weeks or even months until a child appropriates the training and volunteers to use the potty at non-directed times.

4. Finally, even with all your effort, you will still have many wet diapers to change. It can be frustrating to put so much effort into one side of training, only to discover you made no progress at all with the other half—peeing in the potty.

Keeping Your Child Sitting

The single most important factor for bowel training is keeping the child engaged in an activity while she's sitting on the potty. Give her a puzzle or toy to play with to keep her occupied. Opening a catalog to a page of toys or a small book with many pictures will often do the trick. You might also have her sit on the potty while watching a favorite video. That will help keep her in one place, hopefully long enough.

Here we offer some words of caution. Occasionally, a child may show some apprehension to initial release of their stools while sitting on the potty. Patience, encouragement and staying mindful of your child's diet can help. Make sure that you are giving her plenty of fruits and vegetables so that her stools are soft enough to pass without difficulty.

After you review your options, you need to decide. Which path is best for your family—starting with bowel or bladder training? There is no right or wrong way; there's just the way that's best for you. Most likely your attitude is "Let's just get this thing going! *Adiós* tinkle and *adieu* poop!" If you decide to bowel train after your child has learned to stay dry, you will be encouraged by the successes of the moms who helped construct the next chapter.

Chapter Four

Getting Started

*Y*our child is ready, everything's set, and you're raring to go. But, like a traveler examining a map of unfamiliar territory, you see a variety of roads leading to your destination. All will get you where you're going, but each has advantages and disadvantages. Some are wide and smooth, but take longer; others are shorter, but are narrower and have a few potholes. Which one do you take?

From children's books and videos with titles like *Everyone Poops* and *Where Poop Goes*, to adult-targeted material, to the great-grandmother who runs the swim club snack shop, getting help is easy. Information about potty training is abundantly available, and any or all of it can help you through the preparation and implementation phases of training. Amazingly, the advice is fairly uniform and consistent. When we surveyed a significant number of our coaching moms, we found that they followed one of three strategies:

- **Progressive potty training.** Usually accomplished in one to three days.

- **Casual-progressive potty training.** Usually accomplished in two to four weeks.

- **Relaxed potty training.** Usually accomplished in four to six months.

The names of these strategies are descriptive, not prescriptive. They describe how things really are, not how someone thinks they ought to be. Which way you choose to go depends more on your emotional and physical availability and sense of urgency than anything else. Once all the learning fundamentals are in place, and assuming your child has had some success in going on the potty, speeding up or slowing down the process is your choice. The main advantage of taking a slower track is the ease with which you can transition into the fast lane. Whichever way you choose, all lead to success.

Progressive Potty Training

The progressive potty training method is not new. Many of the basic elements in this section were first introduced to parents in the early 1970s by two psychologists, Nathan H. Azrin and Richard M. Foxx, who pioneered a bold new approach to toilet training. Attempting to solve the challenges of training mentally handicapped adults, Azrin and Foxx came up with a sequential approach to helping these people become self-directed in their body elimination. Later, they adapted their research to the training of children and wrote *Toilet Training in Less Than a Day*. While they may not have been the first to suggest the use of a doll in the educational process, they are the ones who popularized the concept. We credit them for laying the foundation upon which others could develop new and expanded models for toilet training. There are four major advantages to the progressive approach:

1. It forces parents to focus on the task at hand—potty training.

2. Because of the concentrated attention given, success is achieved very quickly.

3. The child learns quickly through focused repetitive practice.

4. It is an effective way to facilitate bowel training.

What you need to get started

A block of time. Clear your calendar for one to four days. This allows you to minimize unnecessary interruptions and give focused attention to potty training. This means that you must make arrangements for the other children in your home. Siblings go to Grandma's house, the T.V. and radio stay off, and the answering machine picks up phone calls. Grocery shopping is put on hold. There is only one thing going on in your house—potty training.

Working moms might consider taking a couple of days off from work, such as Thursday and Friday or Monday and Tuesday. Including the weekend, this allows a four-day stretch to give undivided attention to their training. As our experienced moms prove, you *can* get the job done in a day or so. The extra days are for accident monitoring and positive reinforcement.

Snacks. This list is similar to the one in chapter two, but with a slight modification. According to Azrin and Foxx, the snacks needed for this method will serve a dual purpose: for rewards and to increase your child's thirst. A thirsty child drinks more which leads to more urine output. Therefore, snacks should include potato chips, pretzels, sugarcoated cereal, candy, ice cream, cookies, or peanuts. Fruit slices, while much more nutritious than anything listed above, don't create sufficient thirst. Also, stay away from any snacks or treats that are binding, such as cheese.

Drinks. Mothers tell us they find a wide range of drinks helpful, including juices, Kool Aid or its equivalent, or soft drinks. The idea here is twofold. First, what goes in must come out. Liquids increase the number of potty training opportunities during the training period. Second, the drinks themselves are rewards that reinforce motivation. Make your drinks fun.

Equipment. A training doll is a must. The doll allows you to walk your toddler through the entire process from taking a drink with the sippy cup all the way to cleanup. This includes dumping the water in the potty chair into the toilet, pulling up the doll's pants, and washing the doll's hands. (Have wipes available for little people who cannot reach the bathroom sink.)

How to get started

A day or two before you start, head for the grocery store with your toddler to pick out snacks and drinks. Tell her that she can have them in a couple of days. Make sure they stay out in plain view, such as on the counter for the next 48 hours as a reminder of what's coming up—the exciting start of the potty training journey.

Also, no sampling the fun snacks beforehand. If you give in and give her some of the drinks or snacks before the big event, they won't have the same motivational value when you really need them. Also, show her the doll and tell her that tomorrow she and Mommy are going to play potty training with the doll.

The evening before your start date, introduce the doll and walk your child through each step of the process below. When the process is complete, offer her a small treat for being a good teacher and helping the doll learn to use the potty. The purpose of this exercise is to prepare the way for the next day's activities. At bedtime, make a big deal out of the adventure you will share tomorrow morning after breakfast. Involve Dad and older siblings in the encouragement process.

When the big day arrives, your soggy-diapered sweetie will be ready to move into action. She'll need her diaper changed, but for some of our readers, this will be the last time. Don't waste time being nostalgic. Think clean. Think dry. Think happy. Dress your child in training pants and outer clothing that is easily removed.

Your fast-track training starts right after breakfast. Breakfast should be fairly bland but with plenty of liquids. No sugary cereals, syrupy pancakes, or cinnamon toast. Save the sweets for later. Immediately after breakfast, start role-playing with the doll. You have a good chance of success right after a meal, so don't wait. Most children are ready to go, figuratively and literally.

All you have to do now is follow five easy steps.

Taking it Step by Step

Step 1. Take a sippy cup and fill it one-quarter full with a fun drink: lemonade, chocolate milk, or a favorite juice. Just before you direct your child to offer the sippy cup to the doll, have him sample the drink to confirm how "yummy" it tastes. Then, with your assistance, have your toddler offer a pretend drink to the doll. Afterward, take some time together to play with the doll.

Step 2. Wait a few minutes, and with a fun sense of urgency in your voice, have her check the doll for dryness. Ask the big question: "Is your doll dry?" Have her place her fingers on the front of the doll's pants. Of course the pants are dry, so your child should say yes. Join her in praising the doll for staying dry, and follow through by giving the doll a *small* treat that the child shares.

Step 3. A few minutes later, encourage her to bring the doll to the potty. If you're using a doll that doesn't wet, be sure to put an ounce or two of water into the bowl beforehand. Together (because a toddler doesn't possess sufficient coordination to do it alone), place the doll on the potty. Wait a few moments and then make a sound like urine releasing, such as "sssss," or turn on the faucet for real sound effects.

Follow this up immediately by having your toddler check the bowl to see if the doll went potty. When she discovers the water, clap your hands in praise. The doll stayed dry by using the potty, and that is worth a *double* reward. The double treat you offer the doll will be the same double reward you offer your child. Obviously, the doll won't consume the treats, but you want your child to appreciate how big the reward is for using the potty to stay dry. She will catch on quickly to what's going on because she naturally wants to enjoy some of those treats.

Have your child help pull up the doll's pants, empty the potty in the big toilet, flush the toilet, and wash her hands. Then, sometime during the next five minutes, turn your attention to your toddler and move to step four.

Step 4. Direct your toddler to check her pants. Your toddler has already role-played checking her doll by using her fingers to feel for dryness. Checking herself in the same way should be easy.

When you ask, "Are you dry?" your child should put her hands on her pants and check for dryness.

When she says "yes," offer her the first reward. It doesn't have to be a big one (it could be several M&Ms or a fun drink), but it does have to be enticing.

Step 5. You now have a dry child, and you should capitalize on this. Wait a few more minutes (not many), and then have her sit on the potty as the doll did. Success requires that the child sit on the seat from four to ten minutes. Sitting for less time produces poor results. Keep those treats in clear view. Read to her or put her in front of a video to keep her there as long as possible, although never to the point that she gets frustrated. When that happens, the whole day is lost.

If you have a very active child, any initial excitement associated with sitting on the potty will quickly turn to boredom as the novelty wears off. If you come up with a "dry run," don't force her to keep sitting. Three to five minutes is an eternity for an active child. If she doesn't want to sit any longer, take her off the potty and try again in 15 to 20 minutes. The bathroom needs to be a fun place for her to visit, not a torture chamber.

While she *is* sitting, though, let her see that you are holding a double treat in your hands. If she goes, she gets the double reward and plenty of praise.

Remember that the praise is for using the potty to stay dry and clean. Say something like, "You did it, Cindy! When you used the potty, you stayed dry and clean. Let's call Miss Nancy and tell her."

Repeating the process

From this point forward, training is basically a repetition of these five steps. Although the novelty of the doll will wear off very quickly, repeating the other steps will keep the process going, and keep you in control. For the next several hours, you should repeatedly ask the "Are you dry?" question. If she is, reward her.

The Secret of Success

What makes *On Becoming Pottywise for Toddlers* uniquely successful? The type of rewards, (they have to motivate) and *rewarding the right thing*. In our experience, this is the most misunderstood aspect of potty training. Most parents reward their child for using the potty. Given the importance of the potty in the grand scheme of things, this seems to make sense. However, the primary objective of training is not using the potty; it is staying dry and clean. That's what you are rewarding. Dry and clean is the *why* behind your training. It is what you are attempting to achieve daily. The potty is the *how* or the place your child stays dry and clean. Therefore, you need to make dryness the big deal. Dry and clean become the object of reward and not simply using the potty. Once you have your child routinely checking for her own dryness, you are halfway to your goal of successful potty training.

If using the potty is the primary object of reward, the child is in complete control of the process because only she can make her pee and poop come out. When you have to wait until your child uses the potty to reward her, your encouragement and her sense of accomplishment become dependent on her performance instead of her current status. Training then becomes performance oriented, which means that if one day your child doesn't care about going on the potty, the training process falls apart.

When "dry and clean" is the object of reward, the parent is in control of her training. Every time you ask the question, "Are you dry?" you put yourself in a place to reward and encourage without depending on your child's performance. You can ask that question as many times as you think necessary between potty breaks. Meanwhile, rewards are continually reinforcing in the mind of your toddler the importance of staying dry. She chalks up a victory each time her answer to the question is yes.

Time and time again this one motivating factor has made all the difference between rapid or slow success during the training process. This principle applies regardless of which muscle group you focus on first or which approach you choose to start with.

The primary reason why children regress is because parents forget the fundamentals of success. Make it a habit before, after, and between mealtimes and naptimes to direct your toddler to check her pants for dryness. Set a timer to remind yourself. While you will start cutting back on the rewards within a day or so, do not abandon them completely. And of course, always give your child enthusiastic praise for staying dry and clean.

Progressive Potty Training Summary

Let's review the basic steps of our first method.

1. Clear your calendar for 1–4 days to give focused attention to potty training, minimizing unnecessary interruptions.
2. Create thirst through appropriate snacks.
3. Have plenty of fun liquids available.
4. Have your toddler offer a drink to the doll.
5. In a few minutes, ask your toddler to check the doll for dryness.
6. Have your toddler offer the doll a small treat for "staying dry."
7. Wait a few minutes, and then have her sit the doll on the potty and listen for the appropriate sound.
8. Show her how to clean up.
9. Wait a few minutes and then ask your toddler to check herself for dryness.
10. Offer her a reward for staying dry and clean.
11. Have her sit on the potty while you hold a double treat in your hands.
12. When she goes, use praise and rewards for "staying dry and clean."

13. Follow up during the next several days by asking, "Are your pants dry?" Give enthusiastic praise when they are and reward.

It's not for everyone

While the principles of the progressive method can work for nearly any child, there are a number of reasons why this approach may not be the best for you. Evaluate what is required. As stated earlier, progressive potty training demands a parent's uninterrupted attention for one to four days. Can you give that?

Many of the moms interviewed found this method very workable and highly successful when they remained committed and focused on the task. Those moms who were less successful admit that their problems were the result of not clearing the schedule of everything but potty training. As a result, they felt rushed when disruptions crept into their day. In turn, they started to rush their children, and that set the stage for frustration and power struggles.

Not surprisingly, we also found that a correlation exists between potty training success and children who are more prone to comply with parental instructions. Children who willingly submit to basic instructions, such as "Sit down, please," "Come to Mama," "Fold your hands," and "Do not touch" were usually trained within one day. Most were trained within two, and all were trained within three days. That doesn't mean there weren't a few accidents here and there, but they were rare.

More Training Options

Different people take different approaches to nearly every activity in life. Take reading a book for example. In the midst of a good read, some folks just want to get to the end. Their goal is to finish the book, often at the expense of getting anything else done. For others, being involved in a good book is enough. They'll get to the end in due time. For now, it's enough reward just to follow the unfolding of the plot. So it is with potty training.

If a child can be potty trained in hours or days, you might wonder why anyone would want to stretch out the process. Actually, there are a number of good reasons why some parents choose options with a longer training window. We'll let some of our moms tell you why they opted for a relaxed or casual-progressive approach to potty training.

Why one size doesn't fit all

Kristen shares her story:

> I trained Zachary over a period of four months with good reason: Just when he began to show signs of readiness, I found myself expecting our third child. While I didn't want to miss this window of opportunity for training, I knew that I didn't have the energy to see training through while living with morning sickness. I chose a very relaxed approach to Zachary's training. I had a start date but let Zachary set the end date. We began slowly and gradually. I would prompt him at set times during the day, but I didn't feel a need to rush him. As a result of setting realistic expectations for Zach and myself, I didn't get stressed when he had accidents. I just encouraged him as they

became less and less common. I knew from working with Zachary's older sister that keeping him on a routine would allow me to work in specific potty breaks. By the time I was feeling better, he was both day and night trained.

Karen's story is slightly different:

My husband is a rancher, and we have five children. Between crops, livestock, and children, our lives are full and our days hectic. Since I didn't have the luxury of dropping my kids off at a neighbor's or driving them in town to relatives, I found it impossible to give undivided attention to potty training for even a couple of days. With five kids, potty training in our home was a family event, and all my children were trained within three weeks. I know that some accomplish the task sooner, but a casual, yet progressive style of training fit our family goals and lifestyle.

Bonnie, whose 32-month-old son was hyperactive, writes:

My problem was fairly straightforward: At 32 months, Ben was a free-spirited master negotiator who wouldn't slow down for anything, including three-minute pit stops on the potty. I would have loved to train him in 24 hours, and maybe that would have worked when he was six, but at the time I couldn't keep him focused for five minutes. While I knew he was physically up to the task, he had a mind of his own, and most of the time it wasn't in synch with mine. Initially he had no interest in training and didn't care at all that I was passionate about the subject. Since compliance is not an innate virtue, I looked for a strategy that would nudge him toward the bathroom door and onto his super-duper potty. Now, four months later, he is clean and dry and cooperating. I was willing to swap more messes for fewer stresses and take the time needed to make it happen.

If you opt for one of these two methods, your goal and the steps you take to reach it will basically be the same as those described for the progressive strategy. You are still working to keep your child dry and clean, not simply getting her to use the potty. The process will just stretch over a few weeks or months instead of hours or days. Here are some general suggestions to get you started with the alternative methods.

Getting started with alternative methods

Step 1. Double-check readiness. Make certain your family is not in some type of transition or other unsettled period when you begin. If you have just moved, wait a few weeks until the newness wears off and you settle into a daily routine. Review the suggestions in chapter two about when and when not to start.

Step 2. Use a doll. As with progressive potty training, we recommend you use a doll to begin the process. Take a couple of hours one morning and focus on walking your toddler through the entire process, from offering a drink to the doll to cleaning up after the doll goes. Who knows? Your child may surprise you and master the task in one morning. It's worth a try.

Step 3. Talk about the big question. "Are you dry"? Dryness is what you are rewarding. As we previously stated, dry and clean is the *why* behind your training. The potty is the *how* or the place your child stays dry and clean. Therefore, make dryness the big deal. You do that by keeping the question "are you dry" in front of your child.

Step 4. Use rewards. Use the same reward system laid out in step 3 of progressive potty training discussed earlier in this chapter (page 49). This will focus your toddler's attention on staying dry and clean, not just on going potty. Once she realizes that staying dry and clean is the goal, it's much easier to motivate her to use the potty. Keep the snacks out and available.

Find out which incentives work for your child. This worked for Bonnie. Since her son had trouble sitting still long enough to get the job done, she kept a minute glass in the bathroom. Every time the sand ran out of the upper glass (always fun for a toddler to watch because the sand is always moving), Bonnie gave Ben a couple of M&Ms. If he took care of business, she bumped the number up to eight or ten. At other times, she gave him a toy he could play with only while he was sitting on the potty. For all children, but especially for the Bens of this world, the potty experience needs to be a positive one.

Step 5. Use a potty schedule. Have your child sit on the potty at regular intervals: in the morning, after meals, before and after naps, and at bedtime. Don't ask her if she wants to sit. Simply tell her, "It's time to sit." This will help move her toward a consistent daytime routine that includes regular trips to the potty.

A potty schedule is a tool that will help remind Mom when to direct her little one to the potty. It's based on observation. First, note and record your child's pattern of elimination. For example, if your daughter has a bowel movement thirty minutes after breakfast, make that a regular potty-sitting time. If she urinates three times between her morning wake-up and lunch, schedule several trips to the potty during this period. Your goal is to have her check herself and use the potty at the highest points of probability. Observation and a potty schedule can help you achieve these highpoints.

You have heard it said, "practice makes perfect". Going frequently is good practice. Frequency helps the child gain a true understanding of what is happening in her body and enables her to transition to the new sensation of going without a diaper. To maximize successful outcomes, try to keep her on the potty for at least four to five minutes. When she goes, give her a double reward. Keep the rewards and praise coming.

Stephanie Taylor, one of our coaching moms, offers this insight:

The biggest obstacle for our children was getting used to the sensation of urinating without a diaper on. Once they were comfortable with that, they quickly began to understand their muscle control. It was exciting to watch them grasp these concepts and see their satisfaction with themselves. After they understood that they could control the muscles, it was just a matter of training them to tell us when they needed to go.

Stephanie also suggests that while the child is sitting during those between trips to the bathroom, have her sit on a folded towel. Just make it her special little seat while she's watching a video or playing. This way, if she does have an accident, the towel will absorb what the training pants and clothing do not. This simple safeguard can prevent the soaking of the couch or the carpet, and reduces those potential moments of Mommy frustration.

Chapter Five

Bumps Along the Way

*A*lthough the potty adventure can and should be a positive experience, there's always more to the ride than you think. As with many other aspects of child training, unexpected things can happen while you're teaching your child to use the toilet. Here are a few of the bumps in the road you might encounter, along with some suggestions as to how you can most affectively deal with them.

Accidents

We want to be careful what we put in this category. There's a big difference between a child who accidentally messes her pants during a nap or on the way to the bathroom and a child who decides she would rather mess her pants than use the potty. The latter is volitional noncompliance, not an accident. Make sure you identify the problem correctly because one is an issue involving her development, while the other is one that involves her will.

When accidents happen (and they will), try not to make a big deal out of them. If your child has an accident while in training pants, do not punish her. Be calm and clean up without making a fuss about it. Bowel accidents are easier for a child to control than bladder accidents. Most children develop a routine of having a bowel movement at approximately the same time each day (or every other day). When you know your child is due for one, watch for indicators. Taking her to the bathroom routinely and having her sit for a little while can help prevent accidents.

Messes

Unfortunately, potty training messes are unpleasant and frustrating for Mom. There are some proactive things you can do to reduce the cleanup. For example, when you're training your son to use the potty, teach him to lean forward and direct his stream downward into the potty. This will be especially important after you transition him to the toilet. Getting him to aim correctly can prevent a mess.

When he begins to use the toilet, have him sit on the front, facing the back of the toilet with his legs straddling it. That gives him a larger target, and any misdirected spray hits the back of the seat instead of the floor or wall. If he faces the front, you'll probably find more urine on the floor than in the toilet.

Don't forget to teach your son the idea of *tap, tap, tap*. A few drops never quite make it out of the penis during urination, so encourage him to tap the top of the end of his penis two or three times. This will help get those last drops out and prevent them from dripping on his leg or making his underpants feel damp.

Bedwetting

Bedwetting, or enuresis, refers to children wetting their beds at an age when most children are dry at night. It's important to remember the last part of that sentence. Children grow at different rates, which means they achieve nighttime dryness at different rates. Night dryness doesn't always follow closely on the heels of day dryness. Even if that's the case for months, it doesn't mean your child is struggling with the medical condition of bedwetting. Some experts suggest that as many as 50 percent of children under three years of age will battle nighttime bedwetting to some extent.

In the medical world, bedwetting is not considered a problem until a child is about four or five years old. However, if your toddler is having reoccurring nightly accidents and you are concerned about it, consult your pediatrician. Your doctor can discover or rule out any health problems that might be part of the cause. Meanwhile, here are some practical things you can do to try to remedy this problem:

- Encourage your child to wait as long as possible when it's time to urinate. This technique can help stretch the bladder so it can hold more urine.

- As your child is urinating, have her stop and start a few times. This helps strengthen the sphincter muscles that hold in the urine.

- Encourage your child to take responsibility for her wet bedding, but never shame her because of it.

- Consider rewarding your child for waking up dry, but do not punish her for nighttime accidents.

- Consider buying a bedwetting alarm that will awaken your child as soon as she begins to wet. You can find manufacturers and descriptions of various models on the Internet.

- As you move through this process, encourage and support your child while holding her accountable.

Bladder Control

There are two common problems with bladder control in toddlerhood. One occurs when a child constantly has accidents because her bladder is immature. This is a developmental issue. More time is needed for growth and muscle maturity. The second happens because she ignores the urge to go to the bathroom or goes but does not fully empty her bladder. This problem is related to the child's will. In a big hurry to get back to whatever she was doing before nature called, she cuts off the process, pulls up her pants, and then relaxes her muscles. As a result, she wets her pants.

You can usually correct this situation by encouraging your child to take some extra time on the potty. You might have her sing a little song or say the ABCs, and then have her take a couple of big breaths and try again to get all the urine out. If the problem continues, contact your pediatrician, to rule out the possibility of infection, diabetes, or other medical conditions. In most cases, however, this problem is behavioral.

Constipation

Constipation does interfere with successful potty training. But before you rush off to the drugstore for a stool softener, review your child's diet and make appropriate changes there first. Offer her more water or diluted juices, and increase her dietary fiber. Water helps the fiber to swell and expand, increasing the bulk in the intestines and prompting bowel movements.

Here, Dr. Bucknam recommends that toddlers and preschoolers eat from seven to ten grams of fiber per day. Vegetable sources include broccoli, beans, lentils, peas, and spinach. Those might not be the most exciting food for kids, but fruits such as pears, prunes, plums, raisins, kiwi, and apples also have appreciable amounts of fiber. Grain sources include oatmeal, bran, whole-wheat bread, and whole-grain cereals. In the same way, children prone to constipation should limit foods that have little or no fiber, including ice cream, cheese, meat, snacks like chips and pizza, and processed foods such as instant mashed potatoes or store-bought frozen dinners.

If a change in diet doesn't solve the problem, contact your pediatrician and ask about the use of a mild laxative or stool softener. Once the constipation problem is taken care of, you can begin bowel training.

Going Out

Taking your child out in public while you are potty training her can be a little unnerving. Accidents are a natural part of the process, so you want to be prepared. Think about how long you'll be away from home and how often your toddler will need to use the potty during that time, and then come up with some contingency plans.

You can minimize accidents by having your child use the potty just before you leave the house and again when you get to your destination. If public bathrooms scare you, as they do many people, and your car is big enough, consider having your child use her potty chair in the car. Once you get to your destination, discreetly set it up, and move the child from the car seat to the potty chair. Take an extra change of clothes or keep extra clothes in the car for emergencies. Some moms use disposable training pants when visiting friends or going to church, but as accidents become less frequent, you should stop using them completely.

For practical reasons, some parents transition their child to the toilet soon after training is complete. Potty breaks away from home can be a real problem if your child is accustomed to using only the potty chair at home. This is also where a potty seat comes in handy. When you make this transition, at first hold your child in place while you reassure her that she won't fall in. With a little practice, she will very quickly learn how to manage her little bottom on the seat.

Healthy Habits

From the very first, teach your child to wipe properly. (Girls especially need to be taught to wipe front to back.) Also teach them to flush the toilet (after dumping the contents of the potty bowl, if used) and to wash their hands. Start the way you want to finish. It doesn't matter if you are training a girl or a boy, both need to learn to leave the bathroom neat and clean for those who will use it after them. As they get older and are able to use the bathroom alone, hold them responsible for leaving the bathroom acceptably clean.

Chapter Six

Common Scenarios

$\mathcal{T}$he most likely time for parents to become frustrated with potty training is after the process has begun, when a toddler is on the right track and running a good race but hasn't yet crossed the finish line. Potty accidents during this period can be discouraging for both mom and child.

Yet, if you sit down with a group of moms and dads like we did and listen to them talk about their frustrations, you'll discover that their challenges fall into five general scenarios. We have discovered that the answers to these scenarios usually solve 70 percent of the problems. Since the chances are good that the trials you may be experiencing are part of this statistical norm, we have focused on those questions. We believe that the analysis and recommendations below can help move you from partial success with potty training to complete day and night dryness. In chapter seven we take up the most commonly asked questions related to toddlers and potty training.

Scenario 1

A trained three year old gets so engrossed in play that he begins having accidents.

Question: Our three-year-old son Peter was day and night trained by the age of two. However, since he started playing computer games, he's been having accidents. He becomes so engrossed that he has bowel and bladder accidents. We've tried directing him to the bathroom before he begins playing and removing his computer privileges when he has an accident, but neither strategy has worked. How can we teach him to break away from his play when nature calls?

Analysis: It is a fact of life that toddlers and preschoolers will occasionally have potty accidents. Some children have them because they refuse to stop playing when they need to go to the bathroom. But Peter's case was different. The intensity of action from the computer animated characters was simply too controlling. Peter couldn't handle the excitement created by the images, fast action, and sounds. That's why simply removing the computer time for "today" didn't help Peter acquire self-control for "tomorrow."

Recommendation: Because the intellectual challenges of Peter's play environment far exceeded his capacity for self-management, correction required more than just ending the play session on the computer when Peter had an accident. Mom and

Dad needed to reduce his playtime on the computer or eliminate it altogether for several months.

Follow-up: Peter's mom and dad decided to remove Peter's
privilege of playing with computer games and try it again in six
months. By the time the privilege was restored, Peter was developmentally ready to enjoy his games as well as take full responsibility for his bathroom needs. No more accidents occurred.

Scenario 2
A 32-month-old night- and day-trained child begins to regress.

Question: Our daughter Danielle was day trained at 22 months
and completely night trained six months later. Now at 32
months, she is regressing. Danielle is having accidents every day.
What's going on?

Analysis: Even the most secure and well-adjusted children can fall
back into old, less mature patterns, but fully trained children do
not regress without cause. Sometimes the problem is physical,
such as a urinary-tract infection or another less obvious medical
problem. If you suspect that's the case, you should confer with
your pediatrician. Often, however, regression is the result of the
insecurity caused by a stressful disruption of the child's world.
In our experience, the five most common reasons children regress
in potty training are:

1. Strife in their parents' marriage.

2. A drastic change in routine, such as Dad working late or Mom going back to work.

3. A move.

4. The death of a close relative, a prolonged sickness, or a natural catastrophe.

5. The birth or impending birth of a sibling.

In this case, Danielle's family was in the middle of moving across the country. In less than a month, Dad had moved to Cincinnati to start his new job, while Mom and Danielle were still living in the Pacific Northwest. Boxes were everywhere, nothing was in its usual place, and Grandma, who lived next door, cried all the time. On top of everything else, Danielle's mother was eight weeks pregnant. All these events had turned little Danielle's world upside down.

<u>Recommendation:</u> Pregnancy and job transfers are a part of life, and life must go on, but there are two things parents can do to help a child through such stressful times. We recommended to Danielle's parents that they minimize the *variables* and maximize the *constants* in their little girl's life.

The biggest variable to minimize was the absence of Danielle's father. We encouraged Dad to call home in the morning and at dinnertime to encourage Danielle with exciting news about the future. He might tell her about the new zoo she would soon be visiting, describe the boats she would see going up and down the big river, or even give her names of some children who would soon be her friends.

For her part, Mom could schedule time during the day for Danielle to color a picture for Daddy. Then they could walk to the mailbox and drop it in. Mom could also buy a calendar so Danielle could put a sticker on it each day to show how close they were getting to the move date. While such activities couldn't replace Daddy, they could help minimize his absence until the family was reunited.

Along with minimizing temporary conditions, Danielle's parents needed to maximize the constants in her life. The most important constant factor in any child's life is her routine, so Mom needed to make a special effort to maintain as much of it as possible, including mealtimes, playtimes, story times, bedtimes, and even visits to Grandma's. A child's little world is easily shaken, and routine always has a calming effect. The predictability it provides makes a child feel as though her world is under control and allows her to relax.

Follow-up: Danielle's regression was due to the number and intensity of changes she was experiencing. Fortunately, the impact of the changes was temporary. As Mom and Dad worked on stabilizing her world, she began to regain her skills. She still had a few accidents (usually at night), but they were much less frequent. Within a few weeks of the move, Danielle's world again felt secure and predictable, and she regained all the ground she had lost.

Scenario 3
A thirty-eight-month old child is still not night trained.

<u>Question:</u> It seems as though Ashleigh always has to go to the bathroom. Fortunately, he will tell us when the urge comes, and accidents during the day are very rare. But he will soon be three and a half years old, and most mornings he wakes up wet. I am tired of washing and changing his sheets. When can I expect him to make it through the night dry?

<u>Analysis:</u> The first thing Ashleigh's parents considered was the developmental components of the problem. There are four probable explanations for bedwetting. One is enuresis, which we discussed in the previous chapter. That didn't appear to be the case in Ashleigh's situation. Second, Ashleigh's bladder might not have had the capacity to store urine for eight to ten hours. Third, the full-bladder wake reflex may not have matured yet. A fourth explanation (although only plausible) has to do with a full rectum.

If a child has a bowel movement in the morning, his rectum (the storage portion of the colon) fills up again during the day and into the night. The rectum is very close to the bladder, and when it's full, the pressure it puts on the bladder may reduce its storage capacity. It doesn't take much—just enough to rob the bladder of the space it needs to store enough urine to carry the child through the night. While that might explain the cause, it doesn't fix the problem, because attempting to get your child to have a bowel movement at night isn't a workable solution. The rectum/bladder problem is developmental, one that kids like Ashleigh will eventually outgrow.

Recommendation: We assumed that Ashleigh's parents knew the three basics: Limit his fluid intake after 6:00 p.m., take him to the bathroom when they go to bed, and never punish, belittle, or scold him for wetting his bed. In Ashleigh's case, we recommended that his parents give him milk and juices earlier in the day and only water after 4:00 p.m. They also needed to take Ashleigh to the potty just before they retire for the night, or during the night if one parent got up. And, of course, they should make sure that a waterproof cover or sheet adequately protected Ashleigh's mattress.

Follow-up: It didn't come as a surprise to us when Ashleigh's parents discovered that whenever he had a bowel movement in the late afternoon or at night (rare as that was), he woke up dry the next morning. This discovery confirmed that Ashleigh's condition was developmental, not behavioral. His bladder had not yet matured sufficiently to store enough urine to take him through the night. For children like Ashleigh, the frequency of morning dryness measures progress. At first it occurs only now and then, but eventually it becomes more frequent until finally it is routine. In this case, Ashleigh had achieved complete mastery by the time he reached forty months of age.

Scenario 4

A 32-month-old child will use the potty but has accidents during the day.

Question: I chose the casual-progressive method to train my son, Clark. He adapted to the potty chair amazingly fast, but although he receives a reward for using it, he often has accidents throughout the day. I constantly ask him if he needs to use the potty, and most often his response is no. But then the accidents come. Is this just a developmental issue with Clark, or have we missed something?

Analysis: Through a series of questions, we discovered that Clark's mom and dad made a big deal whenever their son used the potty. This included giving him a fun reward and plenty of praise and encouragement. We gave Mom and Dad an "A" for effort and diligence. Unfortunately, they forgot the secret of success: *Reward a child for using the potty to stay dry and clean, not simply for using the potty.*

Following this principle makes all the difference in the world. Like this mom and dad, most parents reward their toddler after she successfully uses the potty. While using the potty is definitely important, it is a *secondary* goal of training. This is where Clark's parents got off track. They rewarded him for using the potty instead of rewarding him for staying dry and clean between trips to the potty.

Recommendation: We recommended that Clark's parents change the emphasis and timing of rewards. Clark had been trained to check himself for dryness, so as often as every 20 to 30 minutes throughout the day, Mom needed to ask him if he is dry. If the answer is yes—which it should be most of the time—she gives Clark a small reward and plenty of praise. When he sits on the potty and goes, she gives him a double reward. This double treat is not for just using the potty, but for using it as a way to stay dry and clean.

<u>Follow up:</u> Five days after Clark's mother began to reward him for staying dry and clean, she reported that accidents were now rare. Clark was coming to his parents during the day to tell them he was dry and clean. Granted, getting a treat was a big motive for this. But with every passing day, the habits of cleanliness were becoming more deeply ingrained in Clark's little life, and complete potty training success was very close at hand.

Scenario 5

A 28-month-old child will use the potty when told to, but not voluntarily.

<u>Question:</u> My son Travis has been a compliant child from birth. When we direct him to the potty, he usually goes without fussing, and we reward him for that. When it comes to doing his poops, he is so regular that I can set my clock by it, so we have very few problems there. But that's only because I can predict when he will go and direct him to the potty. By directing him, I can keep him dry and clean 80 percent of the time, but what

about the other 20 percent? How do I get him to tell us when he has to go?

<u>Analysis:</u> Travis was doing quite well when you consider all that he had to master to reach this level of potty proficiency. He had obviously learned to control the various muscles used in elimination and had no problems using the potty. But in truth, complete potty training is more than that; true success is achieved only when Travis directs himself to use the potty. Travis is a smart little guy. He had already learned that when he went potty, he got a surprise treat. We needed to take advantage of that fact to move him from other-directed to self-directed.

<u>Recommendation:</u> We sent Travis's mom and dad home with the following suggestions. They would inform Travis that he would still get his special treat when he used the potty after they told him to. But if *he* told *them* that he needed to use the potty and then used it, he would get a *big* surprise—a really big one! Mom and Dad's only challenge was to figure out what a big surprise would look like for Travis.

<u>Follow-up:</u> With great enthusiasm, Mom reported back to us that the big-treat motivation had worked in less than 48 hours. Travis began letting Mom and Dad know when he had to go. He would call out to them from his bed in the morning and after naps, and he started coming in from the backyard to tell Mom he had to use the potty. In less than four days, self-directed

potty use became Travis's norm. He was no longer dependent on prompts from his parents.

So, what was the big surprise they came up with? Instead of receiving a few little M&M candies or raisins, Travis got his all-time favorite: two Keebler cheese and peanut butter crackers. This may not seem like a big reward to the rest of us, but it motivated Travis, and that's what counted. In less than one week, he went from being parent-directed to self-directed, while his accident rate went from 20 percent to just about nil.

Note the difference between the problem facing Travis's parents and the one that faced the parents of Clark, the child in our fourth scenario. In Clark's case, the challenge was related to the *timing* and *emphasis* of rewards, while in Travis's case, it was the *size* of the reward that was the motivating factor.

Chapter Seven

Common Questions

*I*n this chapter we expand on the five general scenarios of chapter six by providing answers to the fifteen most commonly asked questions. A summary of the questions appear below followed by our explanation.

Question 1: My daughter Lacey is nearly three. She has very few accidents, even at night, and we are pleased with her success in using the toilet to stay dry. However, she refuses to use the potty for her poops. Instead, every day is another day of messy diapers. What do I do?

Question 2: My son seems to be fixated on food, so when I was training him, food rewards worked well. Now that he is trained, I am finding it difficult to give up the rewards for fear he will regress. What do I do?

Question 3: The rewards worked great, but now how do I get rid of the need for them?

Question 4: Should I train my twins together or separately?

Question 5: Is punishment ever appropriate during the training process?

Question 6: Are girls really easier to train than boys?

Question 7: I'm working with my son to help him urinate into the potty, but his trajectory is all over the place. Help me!

Question 8: My two year old has a mind of his own and refuses to sit on the potty. What should I do?

Question 9: My son did fine when I was supervising his training, but once I went back to work, he began wetting and messing just as if he hadn't been trained. What do I do?

Question 10: My three-and-a-half-year-old son, like his five-year-old sister, wants privacy when he goes to the bathroom. I think he should keep the door open, but he wants it closed when he does his business. Should I insist that he keep it open?

Question 11: How should we handle using public bathrooms?

Question 12: Can I use diapers or pull-ups at night while my child is moving toward nighttime dryness?

Question 13: My child will not sit very long on the potty (or anywhere else). What can I do to help him stay seated until he is finished?

Questions 14: Can a child get bored with potty training?

Question 15: What about videos and books? Are they helpful?

∞

Question 1: My daughter Lacey is nearly three. She has very few accidents, even at night, and we are pleased with her success in using the toilet to stay dry. However, she refuses to use the potty for her poops. Instead, every day is another day of messy diapers. What do I do?

Answer: First, we must dismiss the notion that such behavior is rooted in the child's fear that she might lose part of her body if she poops in the potty. An adult might be able to imagine such an outcome, but children do not think that way. Lacey is not afraid to sit on the potty; she just won't have her bowel movements there. If fear is not the problem, what is driving Lacey's behavior, and what can her parents do about it? When it comes to contradictory behaviors, it's hard to discern what's going on in the mind of a toddler, but there are some practical things her parents can do to address the problem.

First, make sure constipation is not a factor. Next, they should consider this a behavioral challenge in need of specific encouragement. Scolding and discipline will not help in this situation; rewards and encouragement will. Think positive not negative.

We suggested that Lacey's parents take her for a stroll up and down the aisle of their local toy store, letting her look over the selection for one special item of interest, one fun and attractive enough to make it worth her while to go poop in the potty. Lacey should look at and hold the toy, but her parents should not buy it then. Just let her know, with great enthusiasm, that they will bring her back to the store and buy the toy if she poops in the potty for three consecutive days. At home, they can help Lacey understand what three consecutive days look like by using a calendar and star stickers. For every day of success she puts a star on the calendar, and when there are three stars in a row, you go back to the store and purchase the toy.

We cannot guarantee that this will work for all children, but it has worked for many. What makes it work is using rewards to reinforce right habits. Once your child gets into the habit of going poop on the potty, you are three-quarters of the way to your goal.

Lacey's parents also need to realize that acquisition of new skills never proceeds in a straight line. Progress is more like movement along a spiral, which sometimes advances toward and sometimes recedes from the goal while oscillating upward until mastery is achieved. Potty training is no exception. At the high end of the spiral we see Lacey's mastery of using the potty to stay dry; at the lower end we see her failure to use it to stay clean. Contrary to how it appears to her frustrated mom, both are a part of the upward progression leading to mastery.

Question 2: My son seems to be fixated on food, so when I was training him, food rewards worked well. Now that he is trained, I am finding it difficult to give up the rewards for fear he will regress. What do I do?

Answer: Not all rewards need to be tangible (praise is also a reward) and if they are tangible, they don't always have to be some kind of food. To fix the problem we suggest you gradually change the kinds and timings of your rewards.

In scenario 5 in the previous chapter, for example, Travis's mom did this in two steps over a three-week period. First, she went to the local dollar store and purchased some crayons, little storybooks, toy magnets, colored pencils, stickers, and other trinkets that appeal to toddlers. She placed one or two items in colorful bags and lined them up on the counter where Travis could see but not reach them. When Travis stayed dry and clean all day long, just before bedtime he got to select one of the fun-filled bags for doing so well. It worked!

The novelty of the surprise bag at the end of the day became an acceptable substitute for multiple snack rewards throughout the day. Just make sure that what's in the bag is fun for your toddler. In Travis's case, Keebler cheese and peanut butter crackers were among the trinkets in the bags.

The second step was to move from the once-a-day reward to a once-a-week surprise. Using the same strategy Lacey's parents used to motivate her to use the potty for her poops, Travis's mom took him to the toy department of a local store, had him show her which toy he wanted, and then told him that she would bring him back to the store and buy the toy if he stayed dry and clean for five consecutive days. Like Lacey's mom, she had Travis mark his successes by putting stickers on a calendar. When the week was up, the toy was his. Travis's mom did this twice. The third week, Travis's big incentive was dinner out with Dad.

In this way, Travis's parents moved from giving him a small

reward of food every time he used the potty to giving him a more unpredictable, and thus more intriguing, reward at night for staying dry and clean all day. Each reward was different, and the novelty was highly motivating. The next step was to move from providing a physically tangible reward once a day to a less physically tangible reward once a week.

Question 3: The rewards worked great, but now how do I get rid of the need for them?

Answer: Remember that your goal is to move your child from single successes to multiple successes. To do this you must reward multiple successes with a surprise or something *big*—something that keeps your child interested until toilet habits are a routine part of her daily responsibilities.

Meanwhile, stretch the rewards by using a chart. If you search the Internet, you can find a variety of colorful, durable charts with stickers designed to make potty training fun, and charting is a reward that many children find interesting and encouraging. They get to place one star on the chart for using the potty and two stars for staying dry and clean. Eventually, even the chart will lose its novelty, and once the child masters the skill the reward system supports, rewards will no longer be needed.

Question 4: Should I train my twins together or separately?

Answer: The signs of readiness must be the first consideration whether training a singleton, twins, triplets or even more. Generally, multiples are not usually ready to train at the same time, so training them separately makes the most sense. This is especially true if you're working with twins of differing gender, since girls tend to train earlier than boys.

Training a twin follows the same steps as training a singleton, but with a few minor adjustments. For example, don't leave the treats out on the counter in plain sight for a day or so. That might be too much temptation for the twin not being trained. Also, since there will be rewards attached, don't do the practice run-through with the doll in front of the other twin. We recommend that you ship the other child off to a relative or a friend's house for an overnight stay. It's very difficult to reward one child with treats during the training time while a sibling sits on the sidelines drooling. So wait until any brothers or sisters are gone before you put those treats out on the counter in clear view.

What about twins who do show signs of readiness at the same time? If you're adventurous enough to have two untrained bottoms out of diapers at the same time, just follow the steps of *On Becoming Pottywise for Toddlers* with the twins as you would for a singleton. Why not try it? It's very likely that at least one child, and possibly both, will learn to stay dry and clean. If you have success with one, but not the other, you haven't really lost anything. Just transition to a more relaxed or casual approach, and in time the twin will catch up.

Question 5: Is punishment ever appropriate during the training process?

Answer: It depends on how you define the word "punishment." Since most problems associated with potty training are developmental, corporal punishment is not an appropriate or productive way to try to prevent potty training accidents. Instead, when your child has an accident, try following up with logical consequences. Remember Peter, whose fascination with computer games was the leading cause of his accidents? His parents used a form of logical consequence when they took away his computer privileges until he was developmentally ready to play without having accidents.

Other parents we know told us that they moved their three-and-a-half year old from having occasional accidents to remaining dry and clean by insisting that he help Mom or Dad with the cleanup process. However, we recommend using this approach only for a child who is at least three and a half, and then only cautiously and with much patience.

Question 6: Are girls really easier to train than boys?

Answer: The assumption that girls are easier to train than boys is widespread, but according to the moms we talk to who have trained both, the answer is no. In truth, no studies affirm the view that girls are easier to train.

The fact that girls tend to show signs of readiness sooner might contribute to this misconception. Girls typically develop bladder readiness between 20 and 26 months of age, while boys usually develop it between 24 and 32 months of age. Girls train sooner than boys because their bladder readiness occurs earlier, but the training process itself is not necessarily easier or faster. Statistically, once the bladder is ready, boys train just as fast as girls and in many cases, faster.

Potty training challenges often have more to do with the child's temperament than gender. Having said that, we do believe that parents will find younger siblings of the same gender easier to train than siblings of the opposite gender. Without much insistence on our part, our second daughter was trained in two weeks. The potty chair was out, big sister paved the way, and little sister followed.

Question 7: I'm working with my son to help him urinate into the potty, but his trajectory is all over the place. Help!

Answer: Once boys can urinate standing up, they quickly figure out they can control the direction of flow and are likely to experiment with their aim and trajectory. What little boy doesn't want to make a game out of it? We suggest you keep Cheerios handy. Drop a few into the toilet bowl and have him aim for the floating targets. If he's a lousy shot or cares less about making a mess on the floor and the back of the toilet, hand him a damp cloth and invite him to help you clean up. Good luck!

Question 8: My two year old has a mind of her own and refuses to sit on the potty. What should I do?

Answer: Physical readiness for potty training often occurs around the same time that children develop an unrealistic sense of self-determination, which is usually oppositional in nature. If you say, "Green cup," she says, "Red cup"; if you say, "Stand," she says, "Sit"; if you say, "Yes," she says, "No." While contrariness is part of everyday life for a two year old, parents shouldn't give up their potty training efforts just because they might not please the child. On the other hand, potty training is not the right time or place for parents to begin to assert their right to rule. In fact, if you make this the hill to die on, you will probably lose the battle. Before deciding on a course of action, you might want to review the material on volitional readiness in chapter one. Postponing potty training might be the wisest thing for now.

Question 9: My son did fine when I was supervising his training, but once I went back to work, he began regressing, having frequent accidents. What do I do?

Answer: At this point, you have clearly accomplished several things, including familiarizing your son with the process in general, introducing him to the potty, and getting him to go while he's on it. However, your success may have been the result of your vigilance rather than your son's ability to recognize the urge to go and respond appropriately.

In this case, your son's bladder and bowel "control" may well have been the mirror image of your alertness in anticipating his need to go and getting him on the potty before he had an accident. When your vigilance went with you back into the workplace, your son's "control" disappeared as well. Although it seems to you that he has regressed, in reality he has yet to acquire self-directed potty skills. Of course you want to continue to be as watchful as you can, but you should also realize that your son may be weeks or even months away from the level of success you thought he had already achieved.

Question 10: My three-and-a-half-year-old son, like his five-year-old sister, wants privacy when he goes to the bathroom. I think he should keep the door open, but he wants it closed when he does his business. Should I insist that he keep it open?

Answer: When we asked this mom if she closed the door while she used the bathroom, her emphatic answer was, "Yes, of course." It has been proven worldwide that bowel elimination involves personal privacy, even for toddlers. The need for privacy is not derived from parental ridicule; it is a natural endowment of our biological nature. The human psyche has a natural propensity to seek solitude for moments like this. Defecation is not a public event. Your toddler is not running and hiding as much as trying to find a place to do his business away from the crowd.

This may be why some toddlers run to the other room, mess their pants, and then come out and announce that they need a change of clothes. They could very well do it for the same reason that Mom and Dad go into the bathroom and shut the door. When a child knows that no one will see her and that Mom will quickly take care of the mess, her diaper becomes an amenable substitute for the toilet, and she resists attempts to make her go on the potty. The solution is to allow her to have that same feeling of privacy while she's on the potty.

So, if your son wants privacy, let him shut the bathroom door to the point of it latching. Just don't allow him to lock it until he's old enough that safety is no longer an issue.

Question 11: How should we handle using public bathrooms?

Answer: Our first suggestion is preventative in nature. If your child is trained or in the process of training, try to get her to go before you leave home. Make it a matter-of-fact suggestion that she sit on the potty and try to go. If you demand results, your child might feel too pressured to go. Just encourage her to give it a try and hope for the best. If your outing involves visiting a friend or relative, have your child sit on their potty when you arrive. If Mom or Dad is around, this usually is not a big deal.

Public settings sometimes present a challenge. For such occasions, carry a supply of tissues or sanitary wipes just in case the janitor didn't refill the toilet paper holders last night. Because of the stalls, moms can take little boys into the women's room. It's a little trickier for Dad to take his little girl into the men's room because the urinals lined up along the walls are often in use. This might not pose a problem for you, but if it does, Dad should ask his daughter to close her eyes while he finds an available stall.

Question 12: Can I use diapers or pull-ups at night while my child is moving toward nighttime dryness?

Answer: There is some debate about this, but we believe that using diapers or pull-ups at night will not necessarily hinder the progress made during the day. The best advice we can offer is to be consistent. By that we mean don't switch back and forth. Pull-ups are the preferred option if you're not using training pants. If you do use training pants, use a plastic diaper cover to keep your child's clothes dry. When you visit friends, take along extra pairs of underwear.

Question 13: My child will not sit very long on the potty (or anywhere else). What can I do to help her stay seated until she is finished?

Answer: Entertain your child by reading a short story, showing her pictures, or having her recite her ABCs. Or she could amuse herself by looking at a toddler-age picture book or playing with a favorite toy.

A third helpful alternative is to work on self-control training. This can be achieved by having your child sit with her hands folded. Folded hands absorbs excess body energy helping to make self-control easier. It works quickly, usually within a minute or two, and that might be just enough time to make this trip to the potty successful.

Of course, you will not want to introduce this technique to your toddler while she's struggling to get off the potty. It's important to teach it to her before the situation arises. You might have her practice it at the table while you finish the last-minute preparations for a meal. Make it a fun game in the beginning and it will soon become second nature to your child. The hand-folding exercise is a wonderful tool that can be used at the grocery checkout counter, the dentist's office, or during that longer-than-usual sermon at church—wherever and whenever your child needs a burst of self-control to make it through another minute or so. Give it a try.[6]

[6]This concept is fully developed in Gary Ezzo and Robert Bucknam, *On Becoming Toddlerwise* (Louisiana, Mo.: Parent-Wise Solutions, Inc., 2003).

Questions 14: Can a child get bored with potty training?

Answer: Yes, sometimes when training commences too soon, the child will get bored in the learning process and start having accidents. There are two things a parent can do. You can increase the reward to recapture her interest, or you can temporarily cease structured potty training.

Question 15: What about videos and books? Are they helpful?

Answer: It all depends on the child. Many children train just fine and just as fast without any aids. However, if you think such resources can motivate or help your child, by all means give them a try. Just keep in mind that nothing is more motivating than a reward that comes after the big question, "Are you dry?"

Epilogue

otty training guidance leads to better results when parents have confidence in what they're doing. We have written this book with that in mind. Our desire has been to provide practical information, offer some workable strategies, and combine them with plenty of experience to give you the confidence you need to reach your goal.

Whichever strategy you choose, successful potty training is basically a three-step process. It begins with introducing behavioral expectations, moves to teaching each step that facilitates dryness and cleanness, and ends with reinforcing achievement. As part of this process, successful potty training involves seven things:

1. Remember that the goal of potty training is dry and clean.

2. Be sure both you and your child are ready before you begin.

3. Buy the equipment you need.

4. Decide on a starting date.

5. Choose a potty training strategy that will work for you.

6. Use a doll to teach your toddler the entire potty process.

7. Reward your child for staying dry and clean.

If you forget why any one of these is important, read this little book again. Go ahead! It will not take you long, and it will make all the difference. We know these principles work and that with a little help from *On Becoming Pottywise for Toddlers*, you and your child will reach your destination without major breakdowns, detours, or delays.

See you at the finish line!

Structuring Your Toddler's Day

By *Carla Link, Contributor*

Author's Note

It is apparent that a toddler's home environment affects the whole course of his developing world. Unfavorable environments, those that are generally chaotic, void of structure or routine, child-led instead of Mommy-lead, tend to have ill effects on a child's ability to learn and the process of acquiring new proficiencies. While it is true that a toddler can learn just about any skill through trial and error, it is equally true that such a process is inefficient, not only in terms of end results, but in terms of time and energy. In contrast, when structure and routine are part of a toddler's day, learning is enhanced, proficiency acquired sooner, and your toddler's day is more like a playground rather than a battleground — yes, even when it comes to potty training.

While potty training is an acquired skill, and eventually something the child will master, early and long lasting success is profoundly and wonderfully influenced by the orderliness of your toddler's day. Order and routine will always enhance learning. With that goal in mind and to that extent, we are pleased to incorporate one of the key chapters from *On Becoming Toddlerwise*. Carla Link is our contributor. She has a gift at helping moms' bring order to their children's world, and calm to their own. We know you will enjoy and appreciate her advice before, during and long after your potty training days are over.

◆◇◆◇◆

S ondra let out a deep sigh as she watched two-year-old Katie and four-year-old Ben quarrel over a video. She had run errands earlier with the children, stopped to pick up a quick bite of lunch, battled over naps, and now this. Rod would be coming home to a messy house, cranky children, an exhausted wife, and leftover burritos. Sondra bent over as she felt her baby Gregory, growing inside, give her a sharp kick. She wondered in desperation how she was going to handle another baby so soon. As she began to weep in despair she also wondered if all mothers felt this way.

Do you know this mom? Parenting toddlers can be exhausting! You might think you need a spare IV bottle next to your bed. Let me encourage you. There is something you can do to bring order to your life and sanity back to your parenting, and to help you get through the wonderfully challenging months of toddlerhood and potty training.

We start with this single self-evident truth. Most behaviors during the toddler years need to be surrounded, guided, protected, and supervised by the hands of Mom and Dad. A child certainly desires to be autonomous, but is not capable of self-rule at these tender ages.

I had a part-time job while attending college. Each afternoon I went to an elementary school and served as a hall monitor. My job was to ensure all children obeyed the school rules coming and going to and from lunch. The school officials understood that without someone in authority standing there watching, little steps of disobedience could easily turn into giant steps of trouble.

Without supervision, young children tend to choose how they will act based on what they want to do, and not necessarily what they ought to do. Toddlers can no more govern themselves in moments of calm than they can in moments of conflict. This is why parents must monitor their children's activities at home. But what does that look like? You're not going to be a full-time hall monitor for the next twenty-four months. The normal, everyday demands on your time as a mother, wife, daughter, neighbor, and friend will not permit that. There is a way to bring your child's day under your supervision without you lording over the child's every activity. Structure your child's day. Toddlers thrive on routine, just like your baby did.

Structuring Your Toddler's Day

Elaine St. James, in her book, *Simplify Your Life With Kids*, suggests, "Kids who live without structure can develop behavior problems. Frequent tantrums, whining, a disregard for rules, inappropriate or aggressive behavior, constant demands, and an inability to share are some of the signs that your child needs more structure."[7]

---

[7] See Elaine St. James, *Simplify Your Life With Kids*, (100 ways to make family life easier & more fun), Pub. Andrews McMeel, page 172.

We certainly concur with that assessment. The most effective way to provide continual supervision for a toddler and yet provide many opportunities for learning is by structuring your child's day.

To have some routine, order, and structure is to think ahead and plan. Structuring your child's day will eliminate a big chunk of stress on a mother. I often find myself counseling young mothers. I do not regard myself as being old (age of course is relevant to ones view of youthfulness), but I do find myself fatigued after listening to some of the young mothers tell me of their daily plights. I can best describe their day in two words: *random chaos*. Nothing is predictable; nothing can be counted on. Every day is disorganized, hectic, fatiguing, and unfulfilling. There is no sense of accomplishment, except that Mom made it to bedtime and everyone in the house is still alive.

You can easily eliminate much of this confusion, stress, and fatigue by adding some structure and routine to your child's day. Both mom and child will thrive on it. A little planning allows Mom the opportunity to be proactive instead of reactive in her parenting —meaning that she can plan the day rather than reacting to each situation as it arises.

A routine enhances good organization, time management, and provides order. It helps you to achieve your personal goals and your child's goals. Another wonderful benefit of planning your child's day is the reduction of corrective discipline needed. Your child is not finding random trouble because his day is not filled with random freedoms.

Figuring It All Out

There are three natural divisions in the day: morning, afternoon, and nighttime. Within each of these divisions are mealtimes and naptimes. Fitting between these two will be occasional potty times. Most parents have weekly routines and even monthly routines, meaning that some days look different than other days. For example, food-shopping days to your local grocery store might fall on Monday afternoons. Your photo-cropping group falls on Thursday mornings. Then there are the once-a-month reading times at the library, outings with your child's playgroup, and "mommy time" at the beauty salon. Deviation in your routine is quite welcome, but don't deviate so much that you lose all the order you worked so hard to set up.

You may be wondering at this point, where do I begin? What might my day look like? The following suggestions will help you get started.

Setting age-appropriate goals

In their book *On Becoming Toddlerwise*, Dr. Bucknam and Gary Ezzo write: "parents need to refocus their thinking from *how* to handle a crisis to the heart of the matter—*why* are they handling it?"[8] They explain that the *hows* of parenting will result from the *whys* of parenting. Why we do what we do is the combination of our beliefs and our goals in parenting.

---

[8] This concept is fully developed in Gary Ezzo and Robert Bucknam, *On Becoming Toddlerwise* p. 44 (Louisiana, Mo.: Parent-Wise Solutions, Inc., 2003).

What do you believe about parenting, and what goals are set for your children? If your long-term goal is to raise a morally responsible, and academically assertive child, than you may find it helpful setting monthly or yearly goals in these areas:

- **Moral Training.** This category requires continuous education. Moral training develops your child's character through self-control, obedience, manners, patience, sitting, focusing, concentration skills, and relationships with peers, siblings, and adults.

- **Academic skills.** This requires the development of gross and fine motor coordination, ABC's, mathematics, language, reading, and more.

- **Spiritual Training.** This relates to Scriptural knowledge, memorization, catechism, or knowledge of historical characters of your faith.

Once you have set age-appropriate goals, devise a workable routine and use your child's wake-time structure to help you achieve these goals. For example, if you want to work on self-control (and who doesn't), you should structure time for your child to sit in his highchair and look at books. Start with a few minutes each day and slowly build up to longer periods. If you are working on sitting skills, or what we call parameter skills (the ability to stay put within a boundary), you might use a four-foot square blanket spread out in whatever room you might be working in. This is great for any child between 14 and 18 months. Provide a few toys but instruct your toddler to stay on the blanket and play until Mommy says its time to get off. This can be worked into your daily routine two or three times a week for ten or fifteen minutes at a time.

Writing Out Your Routine

The best place to start is with writing out your routine. You will find one mom's sample schedule at the end of this chapter. Adapt it to your needs or start fresh. When you begin, consider your personal and family activities including laundry, housework, husband/wife date time, work schedule, and preschool activities. Make sure your daily plan fits you, and not someone else's ideal.

Take a piece of paper and list for each child all the activities of the week, beginning with meals and naptimes. Then you can add the outside activities, roomtime and playtime activities, and table activities, which might include painting, drawing, pasting, coloring, puzzles, blocks, Duplo's and more. There is also sit-alone time, reading time with Mom, and possibly some video time. You must also schedule in shopping time, lunches with Dad, visits to Grandma, and an afternoon play group. Put it all down.

Once you identify your daily and weekly activities, take a second sheet of paper and divide it into half-hour or quarter-hour increments. Start planning each day. Notice how the weekends differ from the weekdays. You can make your schedule as simple or detailed as you wish. Print it out in color or black and white. Frame it, magnetize it, or tape it to the refrigerator. Its purpose is to serve you in whatever form you create. Have fun.

We only sound one warning. Do not become a slave to your daily schedule. As it was in your *Babywise* days, your infant's routine played a guiding role in your baby's day but it was not the rule of life. Your toddler's routine is to serve you and your child, not the reverse. Once you consider the various aspects and uniqueness of your family, start sketching your plan. Here are some specific ideas and guidelines.

Routine

What can be included in the morning routine for toddlers and early preschool age children? Where do you begin?

- Set a consistent time for your children to start their day. Most parents start around 7:00 a.m. You might start earlier or later, and that is fine. But you must establish a start time.

- The first rule for happy morning wake time starts 10 to 12 hours earlier. Do not let your child set his own bedtime. You're the mommy. You set the appropriate time. Do not keep him up late at night thinking he will sleep longer in the mornings. Rarely does that work out and usually makes for a cranky child and a challenging day.

- You can teach your children to stay in bed until Mommy or Daddy comes to get them. Even after you make the transition from crib to bed, your toddler should not have the freedom to get out without your permission. To help with this you might consider placing some books by his bed, (after he falls asleep) and tell him that when he wakes up in the morning he can quietly look at the books until Mommy or Daddy comes in to get him.

- Assist your children in getting dressed before breakfast.

- Work with them to put their pajamas away and straighten their beds.

- Feed them breakfast.

- After breakfast start their morning routine.

There are many activities that can take place. So when determining how to structure your child's morning, determine what activities fit your plan for the day, such as:

- **Roomtime**—The purpose of roomtime is to teach your child to learn to play quietly by himself for a period of time. This helps him learn to focus and to play independently without having someone or something there to 'entertain' him. For a toddler between 14 and 20 months, consider starting his time on a blanket. (Some toddlers at these ages might still be enjoying their playpen time; you do not have to rush to roomtime.) On the blanket, give him something he likes to do, such as playing with trucks or a toy farm set. Instruct him to stay on the blanket and play with this toy until the timer goes off. Set a portable kitchen timer for five minutes for the first few days. After several days, slowly increase the time by five minutes working blanket time up to thirty minutes or longer. As the time increases your child's self-play adeptness also increases. One last note related to roomtime: make sure you rotate the toys that your toddler plays with. When an object loses its sense of novelty the child loses interest. So whatever you place in front of him, make sure it is stimulating and holds his interest. Rotating his toys will help with this.

• **Free Playtime**—This is when your child has the freedom to choose what he wants to play with. It is still supervised because you are carving out the time slot, but it is free time because the child is making the decision according to his interest. What you are not going to do is to allow him to move from toy to toy every five minutes, but instead to learn to sustain his own interest. Keep his activities broad. For example, your two-and-a-half-year-old might desire to play on the back patio, where he has his big wheel, sandbox, slide, and his toy lawn mower. For reasons of caution, please remember toddlers need to be supervised! Free playtime for the child does not mean out of the general sight for Mom.

• **Structured Playtime**—This is a time when Mommy picks the activity. What you are teaching your child is that he doesn't get to always be the one to choose. It is a valuable lesson for a child to learn early on, for as he matures and goes to school, there will be few things in his day he has the freedom to select. Again, start with a timer and use small increments of time. This activity can include playing with puzzles at the kitchen table, coloring, or painting. It is wise to keep scissors away from little toddler hands.

- **Structured Playtime With Siblings**—This activity can over-lap with some of the others. For example, two siblings can be coloring at the kitchen table or playing in the back yard together or sharing reading time. There will be many hours shared with a sibling, and that is why we recommend some "alone" time for each child. While siblings tend to entertain each other, each child must also learn the skill of entertaining himself.

- **Playtime With Mommy**—A time should be structured into your daily routine, preferably in the morning, when each child receives individual playtime with Mom. Even if this is only ten, fifteen or twenty minutes a day, it demonstrates to the child that he is special.

- **Playtime With Friends**—There is value in having time allotted during your week for your child to socialize with other children his age. When dealing with the younger toddler, it is best when playtime is structured and supervised. Besides having a friend over, you might consider attending a story hour at the library, or joining a small playgroup.

- **Video-Time**—Instead of falling into the habit of putting on a video when the children are becoming restless and whiny, learn to structure a video time when it works best for you. Look for a time of day that is most stressful for you, possibly around mealtime or tidy-up time. The videos used during the morning routine for toddlers, we believe, should be limited to a half-hour.

Afternoon Routine

The following are examples of what might be included in your afternoon routine:

- Lunch
- Naptime
- Roomtime
- Structured Playtime with Siblings
- Video-Time

All toddlers and early preschool age children need an afternoon nap. Some younger than 16 months old might need a short morning nap but for the most part your toddler is down to one nap a day. Of course the need for a nap does not always mean a child will want to take a nap. What a child may want is not always what a child may need. The first sign of crankiness after lunch is an early indicator that a nap is needed.

Most moms schedule naptime right after lunch and plan on a good two-hour sleep. So between lunch, cleaning up and naptime, nearly three hours of your afternoon routine is already planned. Some toddlers need some additional time to fully wake up, so for them plan a quiet activity to transition them back into their routine. This might be a good time for a small juice snack and a short

"Winnie the Pooh" video. Other toddlers wake up full of energy; for this little person a trip with Mom to the swing-set in the back yard might be in order. For both types of wake-up moods, after nap-time is a great time to run errands, go shopping or visit a friend. Well-rested children do much better in stores than cranky, tired ones.

If there are any school-age children in the house, your toddlers will be excited to see them. Provide some sibling playtime or snack time together. Older children learn that once they have given their younger siblings undivided attention, that sibling is less likely to demand it from them (in a manner that will cause conflict) at a later time.

Evening Routine

The evening routine usually involves another adult on the scene—that being Dad. Every couple sets their own parameters when it comes to Dad and how immediately involved he becomes with the family after work. The one nonnegotiable would be couch-time (discussed below). In counseling young moms who find their day consumed with discipline and correction, I find a relationship exists between the absence of couch-time and the increase in defiant behavior. Couch-time provides a soothing accent to family life in general. After couch-time it might be kid's time or dinnertime, but for sure it should be some form of family time.

What can be included in the evening routine?
- **Dinner**—Mom can plan quiet playtime for the children as she is preparing the evening meal. If Dad is delayed or working

longer than normal hours, it is usually wise for Mom to feed the children rather than wait for Dad. The longer young children have to wait for their evening meal the more cranky they will get, and the more difficult mealtime will be. Mom can eat with Dad when he gets home, and if the time is right, the whole family can have dessert together. Remember, evening activities should work towards quieting your children down and preparing them for bedtime.

- **Family Time**—This can include an activity that the entire family can participate in. Dad may read a book to the children, or play puzzles or age-appropriate games. Again, save dessert time for family time.

- **Dad's Time with Children**—Children need undivided attention from their father, even if it is only a few minutes each day. Dad can spend time with one child while Mom is bathing the other children. This may be a short walk around the yard or through the neighborhood, or just going to visit your next-door neighbor.

- **Couch-Time**—It is important that children see their parents getting along. They also need to understand that their parents have a relationship outside of their parenting. We have found that when the husband and wife sit on the couch for ten to fifteen minutes and talk with each other, it teaches the children that Mom and Dad are special to each other. This breeds security in children. Again using a kitchen timer, start with five minutes and build up to fifteen minutes over a period of a couple of weeks. If Mom feeds the children before Dad gets home, then when Mom and Dad sit down to eat can count as couch-time.

• Bath Time—Usually bath time for a toddler is a fun time. Have a few toys handy, and of course, never leave a child in the bath-tub unsupervised. While bath time is often playtime, there must be some limits. Your child does not need his entire playroom in the tub with him. Little buckets are fun, but the water needs to stay in the tub. Also, limit the amount of splashing or kicking. This is the bath, not the beach or his plastic pool in the back yard.

Bedtime

When we start to think in terms of adding structure into the day, the first place to start is with the children's bedtimes. If I were to ask a mom such as Sondra (above) what time her children go to bed, she would probably without hesitation tell me what time she thinks they go to bed. It has been our experience, however, that what time we think our children go to bed and what time they actually get into bed can be two very different things. I encourage moms to write down for one week the time their children are actually settled into bed for the night. It is surprising to moms when they see that it is a rare week that their children get to bed at the same time, three nights during the week.

Toddlers need 10-12 hours of sleep each night. Therefore, if his day starts at 7:00 a.m., then he needs to be in bed by 7:30-8:00 p.m. each night. It is not uncommon for moms of toddlers and preschoolers to think that when their children are getting to bed at 9:00-9:30 p.m. that this is "early." I often grocery shop late at night and I am always surprised at the number of parents out with very young children. Typically, they are whiny and demanding and the parents are usually threatening and repeating in return. It is unfair to expect over-tired children to behave like well-rested ones.

When young children are not getting enough sleep they are irritable, hard to manage, and have little or no self-control. Don't start your day that way. Getting your toddler to bed at least by 7:30-8:00 p.m. each night will lessen the need for discipline and correction. Well-rested children behave better.

If your child's bedtime is currently at 9:00 p.m. or later, begin to work toward your desired goal in 15-minute increments over the next week or two. When we say that a child should be going to bed at 8:00 p.m., we don't mean that you start to put your child to bed at 8:00 p.m. Back up the bedtime routine to 7:30 or 7:45 p.m. Include all the hugs and kisses, story time and prayers. Your goal is to settle him in bed before 8:00 p.m.

Helps for establishing a bedtime routine

• Set a consistent bedtime.

• Avoid TV, roughhousing, and wrestling on the floor with Dad; it will take too much time for your children to wind down.

• Avoid conflict prior to bedtime. This is not the time to get into power struggles. Be directive in your instruction—instead of asking your child if he wants to get ready for bed, tell him that it is time to get ready for bed and go with him to the bedroom to get into his pajamas.

• Whenever possible, hire babysitters when you have to be out at night so your children's bedtime can be as consistent as possible.

• Avoid offering a young child who is being potty-trained unlimited liquids after dinner.

• Consider doing your storytime out on the couch or in your favorite easy chair and not in bed. This is a great time for Dad to be with the child. When storytime is over, off to bed your toddler goes. Once your child is settled in it should only be prayer time and sleep. If you keep storytime in the bedroom, you never finish because the child has no place else to go; "off to bed" helps cure the habit of "read me another story."

• Experts on sleep disorders agree that it is best for young children to learn to fall asleep on their own. Give him his stuffed animal or blanket, kiss him goodnight and quietly leave the room.

• For your older toddler, have a rule that he may not get out of bed unless it is an emergency. Make sure he understands what an emergency is and is not.

• If your nighttime routine has been rushed or your child gets to bed late because of your schedule, consider playing soft music in his room to help him settle down.

A final word about bedtime—when starting to think in terms of adding routine to your day, start with the bedtime first, then mealtimes. You might be surprised at the difference in your children's behavior when they are well-rested and are eating nutritious meals on a regular basis. Once you have made progress in these areas, you can look to add routine in the rest of your day.

Mealtime

America is raising too many obese children. They load up every day on sugar, fat, salt, and caffeine. Please do not be misled. What your children eat will effect how they behave. If your children are chronically irritable, cranky, whiny, and unmanageable, the solution could be in their diet. To get your child's diet under control, feed him at home. We encourage you to have regular mealtimes and healthy snacks. Maintain a healthy diet and avoid fast foods as much as possible. Here are some suggestions that can help make mealtime a happy time.

Mealtime Guidelines
• Try to stay consistent with your mealtimes.

• Serve your toddler small increments of food.

- Limit his drink while eating. Fill his cup one-half full and give him that first. When he has eaten his food he may have the other half. Otherwise, a child will fill up on drink rather than eat what is on his plate.

- Don't give him additional servings until he has eaten all the food already on his plate.

- One of the reasons young children are willing to make meal-time a battleground is because they are not hungry. If you are fighting with your toddler and early preschool-age child at mealtime, then you may want to consider limiting the snacks and drinks he gets in-between meals.

- If he misbehaves during mealtime—such as throwing food, spitting, screaming, etc.—put him in a chair in another room to sit for a few minutes to see if he can regain self-control. Inform him that he can rejoin the family when he is 'happy.' When he is calm, bring him back to the table and try again. If he misbehaves a second time, repeat what you did before. If he misbehaves a third time, then he is telling you he is not hungry enough to behave while eating, and he should be excused from the meal. Possibly even a nap might follow. However, if you let him up to play, then that is a victory for him, and every time a young child gets a victory in this manner, he will not hesitate to repeat the behavior. I encourage moms to have their children sit at the table with their hands folded until the rest of the family is done. Then they may then get up and rejoin the family.

- Work on table manners early on; it is always appropriate to teach young children to say "Please" when they want something and "Thank you" when they get it.

A Word to the Weary

We have provided numerous suggestions to help you establish your toddlers routine. However, many reading this chapter may be feeling overwhelmed at this point. My encouragement is to begin slowly. Begin with one thing at a time, like getting your children to bed at least five nights a week at a consistent time. When you see progress here, start on other parts of your day.

Some people chafe against structure. I was like that. I liked to "go with the flow," wherever the flow was going. But what that earned me was children who were argumentative, whiny, demanding, and not very well behaved. I didn't care for the looks and whispers my children's public behavior brought. I was missing something and desperately needed help. When I was first introduced to the benefits of structuring my child's day, I found it hard to do. It meant I had to gain some self-control in some areas of my life that I didn't want to admit I needed help in.

But today, writing from the perspective of a mother with two teenage daughters and one son in his third year of college, I can speak of the wonderful benefits that came with structuring my day and that of my children. Structure and routine gave me the freedom to do many more activities with my children than I could when I had no routine. It will be the same for you.

It will not always be easy because as moms we naturally wonder if our child is missing out on something. So we begin to add an activity here and another there. Before we know it, busyness controls our schedule. What I learned from my own experience is that toddlers do not need to experience everything over this 36-month phase. You do not need to sign them up for every music lesson, ballet classes, peewee soccer, or kinder-gym. They're all wonderful activities, but your child does not need to experience them all. Too many away-from-home activities wear out child and mom.

If you ask parents of college students if they believe the activities they had their children involved in when they were toddlers and young preschoolers advanced them in any way, you will likely hear that they can't even remember them. Having your children in too many activities too early will burn them out emotionally and possibly neurologically. Pick one or two activities for your child to enjoy and let the rest go. (The playgroup and story time at the library are two of my favorites.) Simplify your life.

Whatever Happened to Sondra?

Sondra let out a deep sigh of satisfaction. Her husband would be home soon, and dinner was almost ready. Katie was sitting quietly on a blanket in the family room playing with her dollhouse. Ben was in his bedroom playing with his Legos. The house was picked up. Sondra felt a sense of calm and orderliness.

It had taken several weeks to get here. Sliding the children's bedtime back to 7:30 p.m. hadn't been as hard as she had anticipated, and they were better behaved with the additional sleep. Ben only napped three times a week, yet he was willing to stay on his bed and look at books for rest-time the other days. Both kids dropped the morning playgroup down to once a week, and the only other outside-the-home activity was Ben's junior gymnastics once a week. The children did not complain about missing the other activities. They didn't care. The siblings were getting along better and even looked forward to the times during the day that Sondra had scheduled a joint playtime. It had taken time, planning, and perseverance, but in the end it was all worth it. Sondra and Rod can spend the rest of the evening as they choose! If Sondra wants to do errands, she has the freedom to do them. She now has the freedom to be a mom, wife, daughter and friend.

Sondra's schedule (next page), looks like this. Take whatever you can use and make up your own schedule from it. Be flexible and remember the first rule of routine—your schedule is to serve you and your child, you do not serve the schedule.

Summary

Years ago, Anne Marie Ezzo did a study on the word "amusement." "Muse," according to Webster, means to become absorbed in thought. The prefix "a" on the other hand, means "not" or "without". It negates an action. Amuse means to avert attention. Mothers too often spend their time simply amusing their children during the many hours of the week rather than proactively ministering to the child's heart and intellect. Parenting takes us down a one way street—and fast. That's because children grow and develop at tremendous rates. There is no rewind button. The goal of parenting is to raise thinking, responsible, autonomous children that who are a delight to you and the community. Such results are not achieved by chance or luck, but by planning. Structuring your child's day can help you achieve these attainable goals. Take some time and write down a list of possible activities that make up your toddler's week. Design a daily and weekly plan around your activities and enjoy the peace that comes with structure and routine.

Sondra's Schedule

7:00 – 8:00 a.m. Get children up & dressed; pajamas put away, beds made; enjoy breakfast

8:00 – 8:30 a.m. Free Play Time (Ben, Katie)

8:30 – 9:00 a.m. Structured Play Time (Ben), Free Play Time (Katie)

9:30 – 10:00 a.m. Video Time (Ben), Structured Play Time (Katie)

10:00 – 10:30 a.m. Room Time (Ben), Blanket Time (Katie)

10:30 – 11:00 a.m. Structured Time with Mom (Ben and Katie)

11:30 a.m. – 12:00 p.m. Structured Time Together (Ben and Katie)

12:00 – 1:00 p.m. Lunch, clean up, read books until time for rest/nap

1:00 – 3:00 p.m. Nap (Katie)

1:00 – 2:00 p.m. Rest Time (Ben)

2:00 – 2:30 p.m. Free Play Time (Ben)

2:30 – 3:00 p.m. Structured Play Time (Ben)

3:00 – 4:00 p.m. Gym Class (Ben and Katie)

4:00 – 4:30 p.m. Structured Play Time Together (Ben, Katie)

4:30 – 5:00 p.m. Room Time (Ben), Blanket Time (Katie)

5:00 – 5:30 p.m. Video Time

5:30 – 6:30 p.m. Dinner, clean up, etc. (Mom and Dad have couch time)

6:30 – 7:00 p.m. Family Time with Dad and Mom

7:00 – 7:30 p.m. Time with Dad (Ben), Mom gets Katie ready for bed*

7:30 p.m. Katie in bed

7:30 – 8:00 p.m. Ben gets ready for bed

8:00 p.m. Ben in bed

*On alternate nights, Dad bathes Katie while Ben has Quiet Time

Subject Index

NOTES:

NOTES:

Parenting Resources

by Gary Ezzo, M.A. and Dr. Robert Bucknam, M.D.

With over two million homes to their credit, trusted parenting authors Gary Ezzo and Dr. Robert Bucknam bring their collective wisdom, experience, and insights to bear on this critical phase of growth and development. From first steps to potty training made easy and everything in between, it is all here for you.

On Becoming Babywise: This book is the first of a six part series that has gained national and international recognition for its immensely sensible approach to parenting a newborn. Coming with the applause of over two million parents and twice as many babies worldwide, On Becoming Babywise provides a prescription for responsible parenting. The infant management plan offered by Ezzo and Bucknam successfully and naturally helps infants synchronize their feeding/waketime and nighttime sleep cycles. The results? You parent a happy, healthy and contented baby who will begin sleeping through the night on average between seven and nine weeks of age. Learning how to manage your newborn is the first critical step in teaching your child how to manage his life.

On Becoming Babywise II: This series teaches the practical side of introducing solid foods, managing mealtimes, nap transitions, traveling with your infant, setting reasonable limits while encouraging healthy exploration and much more. You will learn how to teach your child to use sign language for basic needs, a tool proven to help stimulates cognitive growth and advance communication. Apply the principles and your friends and relatives will be amazed at the alertness, contentedness and happy disposition of your toddler.

On Becoming Toddlerwise: There is no greater fulfillment a parent can receive than the upturned face of a toddler, eyes speaking wonders and a face of confidence in discovering a brand new world with Mom and Dad. In just over a year, the helpless infant emerges as a little moving, talking, walking, exploratory person marked by keen senses, clear memory, quick perceptions and unlimited energy. He emerges into a period of life know affectionately as the Toddler Years. How ready are you for this new experience? The toddler years are the learning fields and you need a trustworthy guide to take you through the unfolding maze of your child's developing world. On Becoming Toddlerwise is a tool chest of workable strategies and ideas that multiplies your child's learning opportunities in a loving and nurturing way. This resource is as practical as it is informative.

On Becoming Preschoolwise: Who can understand the mind of a preschooler? You can! Know that above all else, a preschooler is a learner. His amazing powers of reasoning and discrimination are awakened through a world of play and imagination. Through home relationships, he learns about love, trust, comfort, and security; through friends he learns to measure himself against a world of peers; and through unconditional love, a child establishes his own unique selfhood. The growth period between ages three and five years is all about learning, and *On Becoming Preschoolwise* is all about helping parents create the right opportunities and best environment to optimize their child's learning potential. Now influencing over two million homes world-wide, trusted parenting authors Gary Ezzo and Dr. Robert Bucknam once again bring their collective wisdom, experience, and insight to bear on this critical phase of preschool training. From teaching about the importance of play to learning how to prepare a preschooler for the first day of school, from organizing your child's week to understanding childhood fears and calming parental anxiety, sound advice and practical application await the reader. You will find this resource as practical as it is informative, curative as much as it is encouraging.

<u>*On Becoming Childwise:*</u> Ready! Set! Grow! You became a parent overnight…but it takes much longer to become *Childwise*. Just when you master the baby stage, greater challenges arise. Intellect, self-awareness, curiosity, and social roles are emerging-requiring consistent, caring guidance from you. Equip yourself with more than fifteen Childwise Principles for training kids in the art of living happily among family and friends. Foster the safe, secure growth of your child's self-concept and worldview. On Becoming Childwise shows you how to raise emotionally balanced, intellectually assertive, and morally sensible children. It's the essential guidebook for the adventurous years from toddler to grade schooler!

On Becoming Preteenwise: The middle years, eight to twelve years of age, are perhaps the most significant attitude-forming period in the life of a child. It is during this time that the roots of moral character are established. From the foundation that is formed, healthy or not-so-healthy family relationships will be built. These are the years when patterns of behavior are firmly established patterns that will impact your parent-child relationship for decades to come. Rightly meeting the small challenges of the middle years significantly reduces the likelihood of big challenges in the teen years. In other words, the groundwork you lay during your child's middle years will forever impact your relationship even long after he or she is grown. Included are discussions related to the eight major transitions of middle years children including how to create a family-dependent and not a peer-dependent child. How to lead by your relational influence and not by coercive authority. What discipline methods work and what methods do not work and how to recognize if your child is in trouble.

On Becoming Teenwise: Why do teenagers rebel? Is it due to hormones, a suppressed primal desire to stake out their own domain, or a natural and predictable process of growth? To what extent do parents encourage or discourage the storm and stress of adolescence? *On Becoming Teenwise* looks at the many factors that make living with a teenager a blessing or a curse. It exposes the notions of secular myth and brings to light the proven how-to applications of building and maintaining healthy relationships with your teens. Whether you worry about your teen and dating or your teen and drugs, the principles of *On Becoming Teenwise* are appropriate and applicable for both extremes and everyone in between. They do work!

More Parenting Resources

By Gary Ezzo and Anne Marie Ezzo

Let's Ask Auntie Anne (The Series)

In this series of books we depart from our traditional method of dialectic instruction, (premise, facts, argument and conclusion) and turn to an older and more personal style of persuasion—sharing parenting principles in story-form. Who doesn't love a good story?

Stories are entertaining and provide a unique conduit for dispensing practical wisdom and moral truth that otherwise might be lost in an academic venue. When we read or hear a story we find ourselves feeling for the characters through their speech and thoughts. We often identify and empathize with their fears, hopes, dreams and expectations. Most importantly, from their successes and failures we can learn lessons for life. Stories have the power to change us—and indeed they do!

The *Let's Ask Auntie Anne* series consist of five stories and five pertinent parenting themes. Each story is embedded with practical advice that will guide the reader to greater understanding of the complexities of childrearing and hopefully serve as a friend to motivate positive change.

The beautiful, historical City of Charleston, South Carolina, frames the backdrop for the series. Auntie Anne draws her parenting lessons from the city's rich history and the daily life of people living on or near the Carolina saltwater marshes. Charleston's glorious past from the Colonial period through the American Revolution, the Civil War, and into the present day and the beauty of its perfectly maintained historical district, cobblestone streets and waterfront parks are all woven into Auntie Anne's lessons.

The descriptions of places, people, scenes, and the anecdotal stories in each book are factual. Apart from Auntie Anne, the characters in our stories are fictional but their needs accurately reflect the many common concerns and challenges for today's parents. The authors speak through Auntie Anne's life story to satisfy the needs of each inquiring couple.

Come visit with Auntie Anne. Here you will find a friend, one who connects for a new generation of parents the *descriptive*—the way it was and the way it is—with the *prescriptive*—the way it should be.

In Book One, Mac and Vicki Lake can not figure out why their children act as if they are not loved. Mom and Dad are missing something so basic that even the simple phrase "I love you" falls short of its intended meaning. How well did Auntie Anne help them? You decide after reading *How to Raise a Loving Child*.

In Book Two, meet Bill and Elaine Lewis. Who doesn't know at least one family facing the frustration of irresponsible children? Messy rooms, wet towels on the floor, and unfinished homework are just the beginning. Join Bill and Elaine as they go with Auntie Anne on a journey to the heart of *How to Raise a Responsible Child*.

In Book Three, little do Rick and Lela Harvey know that a lack of security is the root of their children's behavioral problems. Nervous, irritable children acting out at school in seemingly uncontrollable ways are a dead giveaway. Auntie Anne's has a plan for this home. Find out what and *who* needs to change in *How to Raise a Secure Child*.

In Book Four, Clarke and Mia Forden seek out Auntie Anne's advice on building trusting relationships. For Clarke and Mia, the pace of today's family is troubling. How will fathers capture the hearts of their children with so little time? Find out what they wished they had learned a dozen years earlier in *How to Raise a Trusting Child*.

In Book Five, Geoff and Ginger Portier tell their story of how Auntie Anne taught them how to make virtues and values real in the lives of their children. What will it take to create a love for moral beauty within the heart of their children? Auntie Anne provides solid answers in *How to Raise a Moral Child*.